HIKES
of Western Newfoundland

KATIE BROADHURST and
ANNE ALEXANDRA FORTIN

BOULDER
PUBLICATIONS

Library and Archives Canada Cataloguing in Publication

Broadhurst, Katie, author
        Hikes of western Newfoundland / Katie Broadhurst,
Anne Alexandra Fortin.

ISBN 978-1-927099-58-2 (pbk.)

        1. Hiking--Newfoundland and Labrador--Guidebooks.
2. Trails--Newfoundland and Labrador--Guidebooks.
3. Newfoundland and Labrador--Guidebooks. I. Fortin, Anne
Alexandra, author II. Title.

GV199.44.C22N48 2014b   796.5109718   C2014-904717-7

Published by Boulder Publications
Portugal Cove-St. Philip's, Newfoundland and Labrador
www.boulderpublications.ca

Printed in Canada

© 2014 Katie Broadhurst and Anne Alexandra Fortin

Editor: Stephanie Porter
Copy editor: Iona Bulgin
Design and layout: John Andrews
Cover photos: Katie Broadhurst and Anne Alexandra Fortin

We acknowledge the financial support of the Government of Newfoundland
and Labrador through the Department of Tourism, Culture and Recreation.

Newfoundland   We acknowledge the financial support for our publishing
Labrador   program by the Government of Canada and the Depart-
                  ment of Canadian Heritage through the Canada Book Fund.

Table of Contents

Trails by Region

Acknowledgments

This book would not have been possible without the assistance and support of the Boulder Publications team, our families and friends, and the many helpful people of this great island whom we've met along the way.

We send a big thank you to Paul Wylezol for answering questions, providing photographs, and much more; our parents, Brenda and Lindsay Broadhurst and Lisette Fortin and Daniel Trudel, for nourishing our love of nature and adventure; our adoring partners, Mike Wakeman and Cory Bertrand, for encouraging us to take this opportunity and for all their help from day one; the great instructors of the Adventure Tourism programs in Gaspé, Québec, and Pembroke, Ontario; and our dear friends Josh

Start of Lewis Hills Trail, June 2013 (from left; Katie Broadhurst, Anne Alexandra Fortin, Cory Bertrand) *Photo by Mike Wakeman*

Bennett, Caroline Swan, and Jamie Harnum for sharing their knowledge and passion for western Newfoundland and for their unwavering support.

We also thank the International Appalachian Trail Newfoundland and Labrador (IATNL) committee for their ongoing support and the staff from Gros Morne National Park and the provincial parks of Newfoundland and Labrador. We also give a big shout-out to the many local residents who directed us to trailheads, taught us about their areas, and offered their hospitality and kindness. This assistance provided us with incredible experiences in unique places that we are proud to share in this book.

Introduction

After logging thousands of kilometres and hundreds of hours, we have collected and compiled information and photographs to create this resource for anyone wishing to explore some of the most beautiful areas of western Newfoundland.

With its rugged beauty and dramatic landscapes, Newfoundland has captured our hearts. Hiking has always offered us the best way to access many of the most remote and untouched parts of the island.

We have included only trails and networks that are 4 kilometres or longer in this book—otherwise, we would have written something the size of an encyclopedia. Many shorter trails can be found in almost every region, and we encourage hikers to refer to other tourism resources to find out more (to start, see "Further information" on page 169). Each of these shorter trails has something to offer and will help you further enjoy a new area.

We have organized this book along the island's vehicle transportation routes, starting in the southernmost region of Newfoundland, nearest to the ferry docks at Port aux Basques. Many visitors to the island begin there, and the southwest coast is a spectacular place to start a hiking adventure.

From the southwest coast, we progressed north, following the Trans-Canada Highway (Route 1) to the Bay of Islands and the Humber Valley. From Deer Lake, we explored northward to Gros Morne National Park and the Northern Peninsula before heading east and highlighting the trails of central Newfoundland in the Baie Verte and Twillingate areas.

We encourage interested hikers to pick up *Hikes of Eastern Newfoundland*, a guide to the trails from Fogo Island to St. John's and the southern Avalon Peninsula, also published by Boulder Publications.

We hope that our fellow hikers will find this a useful resource and an interesting read. We look forward to seeing you on the trails of western and central Newfoundland.

How to use this book

Our intent is to give you the information and tools you need to success-fully get to the start and end of each hike. We have tried to organize the hike descriptions logically so they will be easy to use. We did not want to write a novel about our adventures—we want to set you up for your own!

Page Layout

Nearest community/ town name (or park or route number)

Trail number and name

Bar colour indicates region*

Rating: Easy (1) Moderate (2) Difficult (3) Strenuous (4) Wilderness (W)

Tent icon indicates an overnight hike; compass icon indicates an unmarked trail (map and compass skills required)

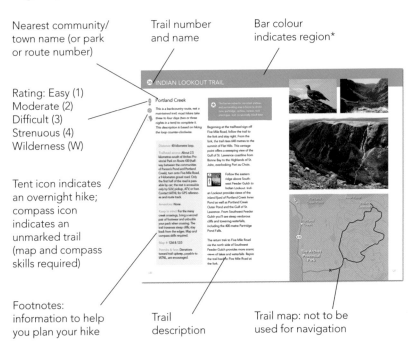

Footnotes: information to help you plan your hike

Trail description

Trail map: not to be used for navigation

*Bar colour key

Southwest Coast

Bay of Islands & Humber Valley

Gros Morne National Park

Northern Peninsula

Central Newfoundland: Baie Verte & Twillingate

More information about the page layout

Trail ratings
The trails in this book have been rated as Easy, Moderate, Difficult, Strenuous, or Wilderness. The first four categories are based on the ratings used by the East Coast Trail Association (www.eastcoasttrail.ca), with some changes to account for the terrain of Newfoundland's west coast and the specific hikes described in this book.

Please read the ratings descriptions below carefully; when we rated hikes, we considered ease of access, duration, distance, elevation changes, trail conditions, and signage.

1 **Easy:** Beginner-friendly trails accessible for most fitness and experience levels. Trails are easy to access and, in general, well signed, range from less than 1 kilometre to 7 kilometres return, and have elevation changes up to 50 metres. Trail surfaces are generally gravel walkways, boardwalks, or footpaths, and trails are in good condition.

2 **Moderate:** Easy-to-access trails ranging from 4 to 11 kilometres return. Trails generally have elevation changes up to approximately 150 metres; these changes will occur more frequently than on "easy" hikes. Trail surfaces are typically gravel walkways or footpaths over uneven terrain, and trails are in good condition.

3 **Difficult:** Easy-to-access trails ranging from 9 to 17 kilometres in length. Expect significant elevation changes, often greater than 250 metres; trails are good to very rugged footpaths and may include steep climbs or scrambles. Boardwalks, bridges, or logs may cover some wet spots.

4 **Strenuous:** Trails are easy to access and up to 17 kilometres in length; however, major elevation changes of up to 806 metres will occur, and for prolonged durations. Footpaths, ranging from good to very rugged, may include steep climbs or scrambles, sometimes with logs, boardwalks, or bridges in wet areas.

Wilderness: Backcountry routes and trails for fit and experienced hikers. Remote trailheads may require a four-wheel drive or boat to access. Map and compass skills are essential; the route may be unmarked. Expect major elevation changes. These routes may call for overnighting in tents, often without designated campsites.

A second "boot" icon indicates a second trail or optional add-on hike, or that the difficulty level falls between two levels. Please read the trail description for details.

Other icons

The trail requires camping for one or more nights. If the tent icon is greyed-out, camping is optional—read the trail description for details. Tent sites indicated on the map are approximate locations and subject to change. Amenities vary with the site.

The trail or route is unmarked and map and compass skills are mandatory. Do not rely only on a Global Positioning Device (GPD), such as a cell phone, or Global Positioning System (GPS). A greyed-out compass indicates an optional backcountry hike add-on.

Trail description
An overview of the hike, describing major junctions, lookout locations, and landmarks along the intended route. It also includes elevation changes, trail conditions, potential hazards, and other noteworthy information.

Trail map
The map(s) included with each trail gives a general idea of the terrain, the location of main junctions and trailheads, and a bird's-eye view of the hike. Depending on the scale of the map, topographic lines are shown in either feet or metres. Not all roads or landmarks are shown. **Disclaimer: The maps provided in this guide should not be used for navigation purposes.** Please purchase a reliable government topographic map for any backcountry hiking or other trail requiring navigation.

———— Road   Λ   Campsite

~~~~ Hiking trail   🗼   Lighthouse

●   Trailhead

Footnotes

Distance: The hike length in kilometres (to the nearest half-kilometre) and trail type (loop, linear, or network). Estimated hiking times are not included, as these vary depending on the fitness level of each member in the group, size of group, and trail conditions. Most people of average fitness can walk 4 to 5 kilometres per hour on a smooth road; that pace will slow considerably on a trail, especially one with uphill climbs.

Trailhead access: Driving route to trailhead, but may include boat access information. Also identifies parking areas and provides the decimal degrees of the main trailhead commonly used by GPS. Be sure to correct for declination. GPS information is from Natural Resources Canada via Toporama and is subject to a degree of error.

Amenities: Facilities or services available on the trail or at the trailhead, including outhouses and interpretation panels.

Keep in mind: Cautions specific to the trail. Please take all warnings seriously.

Permits & fees: Brief information about day passes, permits, or donations.

Map #: Refers to the Natural Resources Canada topographic maps of the terrain in which the trail is located. Map numbers are included only for wilderness trails. Topographic maps may be obtained from a map dealer, GeoGratis website (www.geogratis.ca), a regional distribution centre, or a certified map printer. The Gros Morne visitor centre has topo maps for the Long Range and North Rim traverses.

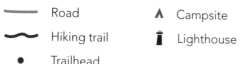

Interesting information: Historical notes, natural feature highlights, geologic information, personal observations, and recommendations.

Further information, including town or organization contact information, relevant websites, or useful YouTube videos, begins on page 169. The information is current to the best of our knowledge and subject to change.

Assumption of risk

Walking and hiking in Newfoundland is inherently risky due to many factors including, but not limited to, unpredictable weather, falling rocks, falling trees, and animal encounters.

This guide is designed to provide general guidelines about each hike. Trail descriptions have been carefully researched by local professionals; however, conditions not mentioned in the hike descriptions may be encountered. Trailheads, signage, parking, and other amenities are also subject to change.

Good to know before you go …

Climate and weather of Western & Central Newfoundland

The island of Newfoundland is surrounded by the Atlantic Ocean, which creates a temperate climate; however, the weather is changeable and difficult to predict.

Summer refers to the warmest months of the year: June to August. These months are generally warm with cool breezes and temperatures ranging from 10°C to 20°C.

Fall is a short season in Newfoundland, generally from September to October, but with cooler temperatures than those of summer and typically sunny days, it is enjoyable for hiking. Temperatures range from highs of 15°C to lows of 5°C.

Winter, the longest season, spans from November through March. November can bring tropical storms with high winds and heavy rains.

With December comes freezing temperatures and snow. Winter temperatures range from -30°C to 0°C (depending on the wind), which can make for mild days and frosty nights. By March, there could be up to 3 metres of snow—on sunny days, then, it is time to play!

Spring comes as days warm in April and by May temperatures can hit highs of about 10°C; nights may still be frosty.

The west coast's annual average precipitation is 1,629 millimetres, while the central area receives 1,182 millimetres; wet weather gear, therefore, is a must any time of year. We have found that Environment Canada (weather.gc.ca) provides the most accurate and up-to-date forecasts.

Tides, wind, and fog

Each day two low and two high tides occur at approximately six-hour intervals. Tides could leave you stranded on a beach or island if you are not keeping track of them. Keep in mind that tides do not always reach the same height; fluctuations depend on the pull of the moon and sun; as well, neap and spring tides are higher or lower than usual.

For a schedule of the tides for specific locations, visit Fisheries and Oceans Canada: www.waterlevels.gc.ca/eng/station/list.

The ocean occasionally brings fog onto the shoreline which can roll in quickly and severely reduce visibility. Fog is particularly dangerous if you are venturing near cliffs or travelling at higher elevations and it can cause you to lose the trail and become disoriented. Waiting for the fog to clear is safer than heading out in the wrong direction.

Beware of high winds by cliffs and mountaintops: they can be extremely powerful all around Newfoundland, reaching speeds of 100+ kilometres per hour.

Animals

Wild animals are unpredictable, even if they appear tame. Do not get too close and do not feed them. Do keep binoculars and cameras with you at all times. Remember that anything odorous in your tent—food, and even toothpaste and deodorant—attracts wildlife.

Wildlife is found everywhere in Newfoundland. Alex once saw a moose in the parking lot of the grocery store in the middle of St. Anthony on the Northern Peninsula.

Moose

Moose, which are native to Labrador, were introduced to the island of Newfoundland at Gander Bay in 1878 and in 1904 four moose were introduced at Howley. The moose population has flourished to over 150,000 due to the abundance of food and virtually no natural predators. Its main threat is humans. Moose is an important game animal, with approximately 22,000 animals harvested yearly. The fact that Newfoundland has the highest density of moose in the world poses problems of moose-vehicle collisions and deforestation as well as the introduction of other non-native species (possibly wolves) to help control the moose population.

Be cautious around moose, especially in the spring when the cow (female) has calves, as they are extremely protective of their new offspring. Females have been known to charge and will trample anything in their path. In the fall, be wary of rutting bulls (male).

Learn to recognize a moose's warnings: raising the long hair on its shoulder hump, laying back its ears (like a dog or cat does), or licking its lips, huffing, or grunting. When you encounter a moose, whether or not it sees you, avert your eyes (but watch it from the corner of your eye), and back away slowly; find another route or return to the trailhead. If the moose approaches or charges, look for the nearest tree, fence, car, or other obstruction to duck behind. When a moose charges, it often kicks forward with its front hooves, so get behind something solid. It is usually a good idea to run from a moose (unlike bears) because they won't chase you far and you can run around a tree faster than a moose can. Moose are not agile—weaving and circling or getting into thick brush usually deters them.

If a moose knocks you down, it may continue running or stomp and kick with all four hooves. Either way, curl up in a ball, protect your head with your hands, and hold still. Don't move or try to get up until the moose moves a safe distance away.

Black bears and polar bears

Black bears are native to the island and sometimes polar bears cross on the ice pack in the winter from Labrador onto the Northern Peninsula. Both are curious and intelligent and tend to avoid or ignore people, but both can be dangerous. Bears do not like surprises, so when you're hiking, announce your presence by making a noise, singing, talking loudly, or by tying a bell to your pack. Never approach or provoke a bear—it could be just passing through, but it could become aggressive if it has young cubs nearby or is protecting a kill, or if you've strayed too close.

When you are backcountry camping, cook away from your tent. Store all food away from your campsite and, ideally, hung out of reach of bears. If the area is treeless, store all food in airtight or specially designed bear-proof containers. Dogs and their food may also attract bears. Always keep a clean camp by washing dishes thoroughly, burn-

ing garbage completely in a hot fire (or packing it out), and eliminating food smells from clothing. As food and garbage attract bears, treat them both with equal care.

If you see a bear, try to avoid it, and give it every opportunity to avoid you. If you do encounter one at close range, remain calm. Attacks are rare. Most bears are interested only in protecting food, cubs, or their "personal space." Once the threat has been removed, they will move on. If you encounter a bear, remember:

■ Identify yourself: Let the bear know you are human. Talk to the bear in a normal voice. Wave your arms. Help the bear recognize you. If a bear cannot tell what you are, it may come closer or stand on its hind legs to get a better look or smell. A standing bear is usually curious, not threatening. Try to back away slowly, diagonally, but if the bear follows, stop and hold your ground.

■ Don't run: You can't outrun a bear. They have been clocked at speeds up to 56 kilometres per hour and, like dogs, they will chase fleeing animals. Bears often make bluff charges, sometimes to within 3 metres of their adversary, without making contact. Continue waving your arms and talking to the bear. If it comes too close, raise your voice and be more aggressive. Bang pots and pans. Use noisemakers. Never imitate bear sounds or make a high-pitched squeal.

■ If attacked: If a black bear makes contact, fight back regardless of circumstances. If a polar bear attacks, fight back unless the attack is by a mother protecting her cubs, in which case you should remove yourself as a threat by curling up in a ball and remaining passive.

The above information is reprinted with permission from the Alaska Department of Fish and Game. Visit their website for more details, www.adfg.alaska.gov/ (Living with Wildlife).

Coyotes
Coyotes are considered a native species to Newfoundland and Labrador; they arrived in the province and extended their range naturally, through their own efforts. However, they have only been on the island since the mid-1980s. Coyotes tend to have a natural fear of humans and are usually easily scared off. Be alert in the woods and watch for signs such as scat or tracks. Attacks are extremely rare and are usually related to a coyote's

habituation to people and their food. If you are approached, it is probably because the coyote has become used to being fed by people. Stop, remain calm, and assess your situation.

If you encounter a coyote, remember:

- Never approach or crowd the coyote—give it an escape route.
- If the coyote seems unaware of you, move away quietly when it is not looking in your direction.
- If the coyote is aware of you, respond aggressively: wave your arms, shout, and maintain eye contact. Carry a whistle and blow it to startle the animal.
- Throw rocks or sticks at the coyote.
- If the coyote continues to approach, back away slowly and move toward buildings or human activity. Do not turn away or run. If the coyote attacks you, fight back.

The above information is reprinted with permission from the Newfoundland & Labrador Department of Wildlife and Conservation website: www.env.gov.nl.ca/env/wildlife/all_species/living.html.

Hunting seasons

Hunting, trapping, and angling are not only a way of life in Newfoundland and Labrador but also a valuable part of the province's economy. Open hunting and fishing season dates are species dependent and can vary year to year. Check the provincial Department of Environment and Conservation website for the most up-to-date information: www.env.gov.nl.ca/env/wildlife/season_dates/.

Generally, big game (moose, caribou, bear) seasons open between the end of August and early October and close by the end of January. Small game snaring and shooting seasons are generally from mid-September to the end of February. Trapping is typically open by the end of October and ends around mid-March. Open season on coyotes usually runs from mid-September through to early July.

Be safe and be seen. Wear blaze orange during hunting season; this also applies to pets.

Trail access

Most trails in this book are easily accessible and located along main roads and in or near communities. Some trailheads, however, are remote and require four-by-four vehicles (most logging roads are gravel and rough); other trailheads require boat access. Furthermore, some trail-heads may not be accessible when there is a heavy snowpack (unless you have access to a snowmobile) and/or early in spring due to washed-out roads or high streams and rivers. When travelling on logging roads, be prepared with extra fuel, backcountry maps, a GPS, and the tools to get you out of unexpected situations (a winch, shovel, tire repair kit, tow straps, air compressor, etc.).

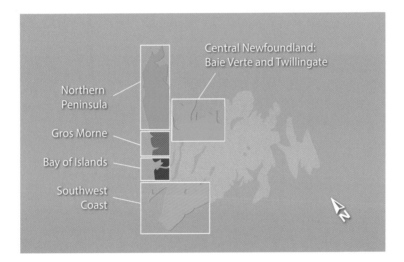

Planning your hike

Area overview

The island of Newfoundland covers 111,390 square kilometres and has 9,656 kilometres of coastline. It is Canada's fourth largest island and the 16th largest island in the world. Western Newfoundland spans 750 kilometres from Port aux Basques in the south to L'Anse aux Meadows in the north. This region holds two UNESCO World Heritage Sites and the International Appalachian Trail of Newfoundland & Labrador.

Central Newfoundland is known worldwide for its proximity to Iceberg Alley, and there is no better way to see these majestic beauties than when hiking along the coast.

The trails throughout these regions vary widely but, like all Newfoundland and Labrador trails, they have one thing in common: there is lots of room to breathe.

Getting to Newfoundland

Since Newfoundland is an island, you will have to take a ferry or airplane to get there. Many people who visit and intend to hike prefer to drive; they take the ferry from North Sydney, Nova Scotia, to Port aux Basques, Newfoundland.

If you are flying to the island and plan to visit the west coast or central regions, it is best to arrive at either Deer Lake or Gander airports. At either airport, you can rent a car—be sure to book rentals early. You may also fly into St. John's, but be sure to factor the day-long drive to the west coast into your travel planning.

Visit the provincial Department of Tourism website (www.newfoundland-labrador.com) for up-to-date information about travelling to the island, accommodations, attractions, and more.

Preparing to hike

Venturing out into the wilderness requires preparation and planning. Some things to consider:

■ Which trail will you hike? Using the ratings given for each trail, determine which hikes are suitable by considering how long you can comfortably hike, the terrain you prefer, what you want to see, and how you will get to the trailhead.
■ When will you hike? It is always best to start hiking as early in the day as possible so you can be off the trail well before darkness sets in. Consider the weather—does the forecast call for rain or other unpleasant weather? Will it be windy? When is high/low tide?

■ Who are your hiking partners? Answering this will also determine which hike you do and when you can go. Be aware of the abilities and limitations of all group members, and remember you're only as fast as your slowest person.

■ Do you have a route plan? It is good practice to prepare a brief route plan, particularly before backcountry hikes, and leave it with a reliable person. Include the trail name, intended route with GPS reference points, start time, expected hike duration, the hikers' names, and a brief description of clothing and tent. At the very least, you should always tell someone where you are going and when you expect to be back, and then stick to the plan. For overnight or multi-day treks, a route plan is an excellent way to plan your trek and can be a valuable asset should you require assistance.

■ What will you bring? For sample basic equipment checklists for day hikes and multi-day hikes, see pages 165 and 166.

Ferries and boat transportation

For provincial ferry services and schedules, contact the Marine Services Division of the provincial Department of Transportation and Works (www.tw.gov.nl/ferryservices or (888) 638-5454).

Reservations for the Western Brook Pond boat tour (the boat transports hikers to the trailhead of the Long Range Traverse and the North Rim Traverse) can be made with Bon Tours at www.bontours.ca or (888) 458-2016 or (709) 458-2016.

Other trailheads may require a boat to access. Contact IATNL for information: www.iatnl.com.

Communication devices

Many cell phones will work in Newfoundland, some even in remote areas; however, gullies and mountains can block reception. Check with your cell phone provider to see their coverage area maps and never rely solely on cell phones when hiking in the backcountry. More remote communities do not have any cell phone coverage at all. When hiking in remote areas, marine radios, satellite phones, or SPOT GPS Messengers can be handy in case of an emergency. Marine radios offer the widest range of reception all around the coast and a coast-guard-specific channel. They are also the most reliable and cost-effective communication devices.

Always tell someone where you are going, when you will return, and what to do if you don't show up within a specified time range (whom to contact in case of emergency and for what/whom they are looking).

Hiking with pets

Pets are allowed within most national and provincial park boundaries; however, some trails (for example, Gros Morne Mountain) do not permit dogs due to the delicate nature of the mountaintop. Check with specific parks about their current policies.

Pets should always be leashed when hiking on busy trails out of respect for other users and especially when you're near a community. Clean up after your pet—no one likes dog poop on the trails. Some backcountry trails are ideal for letting your dog run free: keep in mind that your pet may disturb the wildlife and Conservation Officers can fine you for this. Wild animals are unpredictable; a moose or bear may charge your dog if the dog has disturbed it. A blaze orange vest for your dog is an excellent idea, especially during open hunting season for coyotes.

Practice the Leave No Trace Principles

Whether you are hiking in Newfoundland or any other place around the world, you should apply the Leave No Trace Principles. They are meant to protect and preserve the environment. Always carry in everything you need for your trip and carry out all of your garbage and belongings. Take pictures of what you see and/or find instead of bringing it back with you. These principles include:

- Plan ahead and prepare
- Travel and camp on durable surfaces
- Dispose of waste properly

- Leave what you find
- Minimize campfire impacts
- Respect wildlife
- Be considerate of other visitors

For details of these seven principles and how to apply them, visit www.leavenotrace.ca.

Geocaching

Geocaching is an excellent way to get involved with hiking or entice young adventurers onto the trails. Geocaching is a real-world, outdoor treasure-hunting game using GPS-enabled devices. To play, participants navigate to a specific set of GPS coordinates and then attempt to find the geocache (container) hidden at that location. There are a few fair-play rules, but it's easy to get started and an excellent activity for all ages and abilities. Visit www.geocaching.com for full details, including maps of the areas you wish to explore.

Newfoundland T'Railway Provincial Park:
A section of the Trans Canada Trail

Once completed, the Trans Canada Trail will connect St. John's, Newfoundland, to Victoria, British Columbia, and eventually lead up to Tuktoyaktuk, Northwest Territories, and, at 22,000 kilometres, will be the world's longest trail network.

The railway in Newfoundland was decommissioned in 1988 and the railbed was repurposed as a multi-use trail. Frequented by hikers, snowshoers, cross-country skiers, ATVs, and snowmobiles, the trail provides access to almost all parts of Newfoundland. Like many other sections of decommissioned railway in Canada, this section—the 833 kilometres of railbed linking St. John's to Channel-Port aux Basques—became part of the Trans Canada Trail. We did not include the T'Railway in the hikes in this book due to its size and many uses. More information and interactive maps can be found on the Trans Canada Trail and Newfoundland T'Railway websites (www.tctrail.ca, www.trailway.ca).

The Newfoundland section of the Trans Canada Trail is maintained by the Newfoundland T'Railway Council and the provincial government. Maintenance is also supported by donations and volunteer work.

International Appalachian Trail (IAT)

 IAT is the extension of the Appalachian Trail (AT) located in the United States; it stretches along the east coast from Georgia to Maine. These trails were designed to showcase the Appalachian Mountains.

IAT links the AT to the rest of the Appalachian Mountain range. Beginning in Maine, IAT enters eastern Canada in New Brunswick, crosses into the Gaspé Peninsula in Quebec, heads back into New Brunswick, across Prince Edward Island, then traverses Cape Breton in Nova Scotia, and finishes its Canadian section in Western Newfoundland. IAT also has trails in Greenland, Iceland, the Faroe Islands, Norway, Sweden, Denmark, the Netherlands, England, Scotland, Ireland, Wales, Spain, France, Portugal, and Morocco.

The Appalachian Mountains are found on different continents due to the formation of the supercontinent Pangaea. During several mountain-building events spanning from 470 to 250 million years ago, the Acadian orogeny formed the northern Appalachians and the Alleghanian orogeny formed the section that spans from Alabama to Canada.

The building of these trails would not be possible without volunteers and donations. Kilometres of trail are added every year. Please help IAT continue to flourish by visiting their website www.iat-sia.org or our local chapter, the International Appalachian Trail of Newfoundland and Labrador, at www.iatnl.com. Annual memberships start at $15.

SOUTHWEST COAST

The southwest coast of Newfoundland spans from Port aux Basques to the Lewis Hills and includes Burgeo and the Port au Port Peninsula. The landscape offers a shifting palette of colours: ancient orange mountains, dense green forests, and shades of blue and grey in the ever-changing ocean and sky. The vibrant scenery is the perfect backdrop for leisurely beach walks or adventurous multi-day treks.

Sheltered by the Long Range Mountains, this region has milder weather than the rest of the island. The Codroy Valley holds traditional farmlands and a large estuary to which thousands of birds migrate every year. You'll also find some of the province's most dramatic cliffside lighthouses, such as the Rose Blanche lighthouse, made of granite, or the Cape Anguille lighthouse, perched at the westernmost point of Newfoundland.

The southwest coast is home to the first section of the International Appalachian Trail of Newfoundland and Labrador (IATNL). The International Appalachian Trail (IAT) spans from Mount Katahdin in Maine through eastern Canada and western Newfoundland, to Greenland and Iceland, and, finally, into Europe. IAT is constantly expanding; its aim is to have a system of trails that connects all countries with a section of the ancient Appalachian Mountain chain. Some of the hikes in this region, such as the Grand Codroy Way, the Indian Head Range Trail, and the Lewis Hills Trail, are part of the IATNL, and may require camping. The IATNL routes bring hikers to remote areas and incredible views that only the most adventurous experience.

Trails of the Southwest Coast

1. Harvey Trail / Isle aux Morts
2. Grand Bay West Trailway / Grand Bay West
3. Table Mountain Trail / Cape Ray
4. Grand Codroy Way / Cape Ray–Tompkins
5. Starlight Trail / Tompkins
6. Cow Hill & Beach Trail / Burgeo (Sandbanks Provincial Park)
7. Boutte du Cap & Breadcrumbs Trails / Cape St. George
8. Gravels Walking Trails / Port au Port West
9. Indian Head Range Trail / Noels Pond–Stephenville Crossing
10. Lewis Hills Trail / Cold Brook–Serpentine Lake
11. Erin Mountain Trail / Barachois Provincial Park

Isle aux Morts

The Harvey Trail starts from the Isle aux Morts craft store, a small red building at the end of Cemetery Road. Well-maintained and fairly easy to walk on, the trail follows the gently rolling shoreline. Hikers will experience little elevation gain.

Several small trail offshoots lead from the main trail down to the water's edge, often to secluded coves and beaches which are

> ★ Panels along the trail tell the story of the Harvey family and their Newfoundland dog, Hairyman, who saved almost 200 lives in two daring rescues in the early 1800s.

worth exploring if you have time. At the highest point, a gazebo gives hikers a 360-degree view of the Gulf of the St. Lawrence and Cabot Strait, and the picturesque community of Isle aux Morts. No large trees grow on this barren coastal lowland, and visibility is excellent (weather permitting); this is an ideal location to photograph seaside panoramas.

At the trail's farthest point is its highlight: a mural of local heroes, the Harvey family. From the mural, the trail loops back toward town and returns to the parking area and craft store.

Distance: 4-kilometre loop.

Trailhead: Follow Route 470 east to Isle aux Morts. Turn right on LeGallais Street, left on Water Street East, then left at Cemetery Road. Drive until the road changes to gravel and turn right before the gate, and park. The red building is the craft store and the trailhead: 47.5846, -58.9682.

Amenities: Craft shop, visitor centre, picnic tables, gazebos, café, and outhouses. Guided tours available.

Keep in mind: Be aware of slippery rocks, tides, and ocean waves.

Permits & fees: Donations toward trail upkeep are payable to the Town of Isle aux Morts.

GRAND BAY WEST TRAILWAY

2

Grand Bay West

1

From the Kyle Lane trailhead, the Grand Bay West Trailway begins as a boardwalk along white sand beaches and delicate sand dunes and transitions into a gravel walkway at the barrens. Along the gravel section are platforms with playground equipment and viewpoints overlooking the Gulf of St. Lawrence—this is a beautiful spot to watch the sun set.

The endangered piping plover lives in this area. Respect its habitat and stay on the trail. Many ships have been wrecked off this coast; look for the interpretation panels that tell their stories.

The trail meanders along the shoreline and arrives at an old barn and some family gardens, which are still maintained. After rounding the barn, you may either follow the four-wheeler trail straight back to the Kyle Lane parking area to complete the small loop or stay to the left and continue down the trail along the beach.

If you opt for the beach route, you'll be rewarded with views of the coast and the Long Range Mountains. This trail will bring you to the Grand Bay Road West parking area. Return to Kyle Lane via Grand Bay Road West to complete a loop or walk back along the trail.

Distance: 6-kilometre trail network.

Trailhead access:

There are two trailheads:

■ Exit TCH at Grand Bay Road West. Drive through the community of Grand Bay West, and turn right onto Kyle Lane. Drive to the end, and park: 47.5831596, -59.1844214.

■ Grand Bay Road West, about 1 kilometre from TCH: 47.5960168, -59.184591.

Amenities: Interpretation panels, play equipment.

Keep in mind: This hike is in the Channel-Port aux Basques Municipal Wetland Stewardship Zone; stay on established trails.

Permits & fees: Donations toward trail upkeep are payable to the Town of Channel-Port aux Basques.

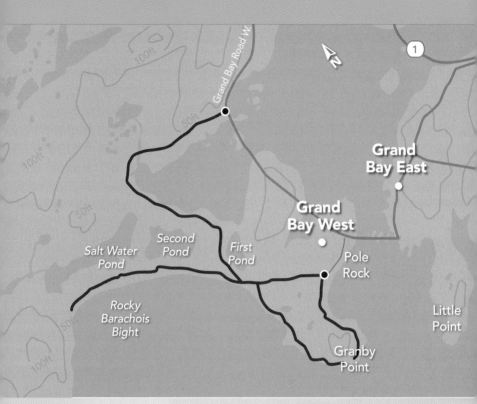

③ Cape Ray

The Table Mountain Trail follows a winding gravel road up a steep, narrow valley. A smooth climb, it leads to a set of communication towers, at an elevation of approximately 425 metres, overlooking Newfoundland's southwest coast and the Gulf of St. Lawrence.

⭐ Local resident Lauchie MacDougall ("the human wind gauge") was reputed to have accurately predicted weather changes. He was even hired to inform the railway company if trains could safely pass, a service he performed from 1935 until his death in 1965.

 As you cross the plateau, the trail changes from a gravel road to a quad track. At the fork, you may go either way to reach the lookouts, but most hikers go to the right. On a clear day you'll see the Codroy Valley to the north, Port aux Basques to the south, Cape Ray, and the lowlands, known as the Wreckhouse, due west. The Wreckhouse is infamous for hurricane-force winds that historically blew trains off the tracks, and still periodically blow transport trucks off the road.

Long Range Mountains

Wreckhouse

Big Pond

Cook Stone

1400ft

1250ft

750ft

1000ft

250ft

1

Billys Pond

Sugar Loaf

500ft

650ft

350ft

Red Rock Point

To Cape Ray

150ft

As you climb out of the valley, you'll probably feel the winds. Imagine the full force of Wreckhouse winds and the importance of MacDougall's role in transporting supplies across the island.

Return via the same road and enjoy the view of Sugar Loaf Mountain and the surrounding lowlands and ponds as you descend.

Distance: 5-kilometre linear trail (10-kilometre return).

Trailhead access: The gravel road intersects with TCH 0.3 kilometres north of the Cape Ray exit. Park either on the east side of TCH or drive in the road, over a small bridge, and park across from the cabin: 47.6641897, -59.2766323.

Amenities: None.

Keep in mind: In an area notorious for high winds, be cautious of changing weather when up on the mountain.

Permits & fees: Donations toward trail upkeep are payable to IATNL. Annual memberships start at $15.

Note: This trail can be combined with Grand Codroy Way (hike #4) for an overnight hike.

Cape Ray–Tompkins

*This is a backcountry route, **not** a maintained trail; most hikers take two or three days (one or two nights in a tent) to complete it.*

The Grand Codroy Way follows the barren, high country between the Table Mountain Trail (hike #3) in the south and Starlight Trail (hike #5) in the north.

This scenic route follows the cliff edge, allowing for panoramic views of the vibrant Codroy estuary before heading inland to the high, rolling grasslands above the Grand Codroy River Valley. The Codroy estuary hosts over 150 identified bird species, including 19 species of waterfowl, which you can learn more about at the Codroy Valley International Wetlands Interpretation Centre.

Starting from the Table Mountain Trail, this route will take you across the barren plateau of the Long Range Mountains—the perfect habitat for caribou, Arctic hare, and black bears— and beside vistas of green gulches and numerous waterfalls. It finishes at Campbells Lake, where you descend via the Starlight Trail into the Little Codroy River Valley, near Tompkins.

Farley Mowat speculated in his book *The Farfarers: Before the Norse* (2000 that these high, fertile grasslands wer once used by the Alban people to gra cattle and winter inland, away from shores that became increasingly hosti as the Vikings pushed south.

Distance: 32-kilometre linear trail.

Trailhead access:
There are two trailheads:

■ The southern trailhead is on the east side of TCH, 0.3 kilometres north of exit to Cape Ray (Table Mountain Trail, hike #3): 47.6641897, -59.2766323.

■ The northern trailhead is off TCH, just south of Tompkins (Starlight Trail, hike #5): 47.7829781, -59.2330455.

Amenities: Codroy Valley International Wetlands Interpretation Centre is located on Route 406 in Upper Ferry; no amenities on trail.

Keep in mind: This area is notorious for high winds and thick, low-lying fog; be alert to changeable weather in the mountains. This is not a marked route: map and compass skills are required, as is a government-issued topographic map. Contact IATNL for a GPS track of the route, bu do not rely solely on GPS.

Permits & fees: Donations toward trai upkeep are payable to IATNL.

Map #: 11014 and 11011

Tompkins

The Starlight Trail starts gently, taking you over boardwalks through forest. After 1 kilometre or so, you'll begin to climb up along the side of the mountain. The ascent is gorgeous, offering multiple viewpoints of the ocean and Little Codroy River Valley from a height of about 360 metres. Be sure to take a break and absorb the view!

> Table Mountain is part of the Anguille Mountains, which belong to the Long Range Mountains that span the entire west coast of Newfoundland. The Long Range Mountains belong to the greater Appalachian Mountain Range, which formed during the middle Ordovician Period, about 496–440 million years ago.

The trail eventually forks, and signs indicate "Mountain Trail" to the left and "Campbells Lake" to the right. If you stay left, the trail will continue to climb through meadows and barrens, finally leading to a flat summit area from which you'll see a breathtaking gorge, lush with vegetation, surrounding Campbells Lake. This is an ideal place for a snack or picnic and pictures and is where most hikers turn around.

Experienced hikers may decide to explore northward: approximately 3.5 kilometres farther is a gorge with a waterfall and sheer cliffs. A topographic map and compass are recommended if you wish to extend your hike to the gorge; there is no marked trail.

Return via the same route to the parking area.

Distance: 3-kilometre linear trail (6-kilometre return) to summit.

Trailhead access: On the east side of TCH, just south of Tompkins, is a large parking area with a trail map for IATNL and Starlight Trail: 47.7829781, -59.2330455.

Amenities: A small shelter in the parking area.

Keep in mind: If you explore the mountaintop, be advised that there are no trails. You must have good orientation skills, a map, and a compass. Weather may change rapidly, and thick fog can disorient hikers.

Permits & fees: Donations toward trail upkeep are payable to IATNL.

Map #: 11014

Note: This trail can be combined with Grand Codroy Way (hike #4) for an overnight hike.

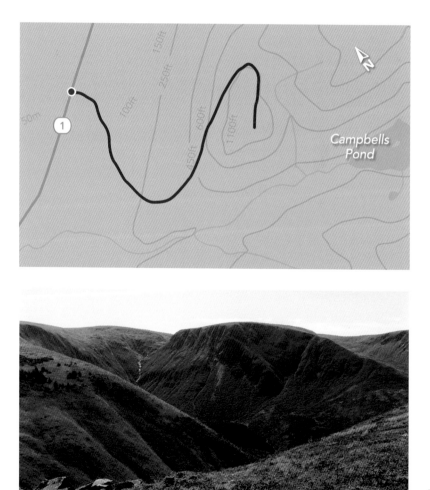

Burgeo (Sandbanks Provincial Park)

Distance:
7-kilometre trail network.

Trailhead access: In Burgeo, turn right onto Main Street, right onto Messieurs Road, and right again on Park Road and drive into Sandbanks Provincial Park. Park in the day-use parking area: 47.6073806, -57.6454407.

Amenities: Washrooms, tent areas, picnic tables, beach volleyball court, and play-ground equipment; benches and garbage bins along trails.

Keep in mind: Smoking is not permitted. All pets must be kept on leash. Sand dunes are an extremely delicate environment; stay on established trails.

Permits & fees: $5 per vehicle daily permit fee or $20 seasonal permit.

Head to Sandbanks Provincial Park and wander the 7 kilometres of white sand beaches. The soft sand will make you feel like you're in the tropics … until you step into the very refreshing water! Climb the stairs to the summit of Cow Hill and enjoy the 360-degree view of Burgeo and surrounding islands while you pick raspberries. If you visit near the end of summer, you may be lucky and find bakeapples.

The trail network starts between campsites D13 and A15, and between A17 and C19. You'll walk on a variety of surfaces, including boardwalks, bridges, stairs, beach, and small footpaths. You can also sea kayak along the whole park and rest at one of its many quiet beaches.

Don't forget your binoculars—watch for sandpipers, plovers, and, especially in the fall, migrating ducks and geese.

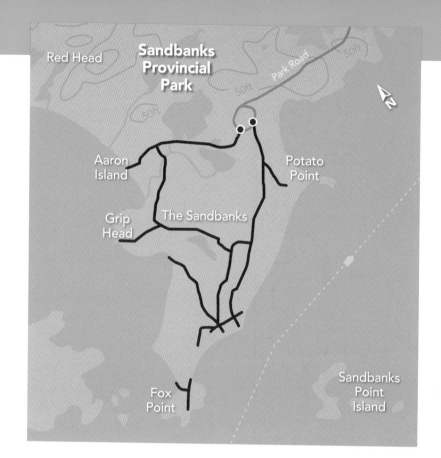

Sandbanks Provincial Park

Red Head

Park Road

50ft

50ft

Aaron Island

Potato Point

Grip Head

The Sandbanks

Fox Point

Sandbanks Point Island

N

The park showcases outstanding ecological diversity. You'll see peat bogs, boreal forest, delicate sand dunes, ponds, and rocky tidal pools—something to satisfy hikers of all ages, abilities, and interests.

★ An abandoned cemetery on Fox Point at the tip of the peninsula is all that remains on the grounds of an old church that was built in the 1880s by Reverend Blackmore. It was blown down by a gale only one year after being built.

Cape St. George

The Port au Port Peninsula is the cradle of Newfoundland and Labrador's francophone culture. The first French fishermen settled there centuries ago; many of the peninsula's communities have French names, and many local residents speak French.

The Breadcrumb Trail is an easy, flat trail of less than a kilometre that leads hikers along the cliff edge from which whales and a rich diversity of seabirds can be observed. Seascape views await; try this trail during sunset.

Hikers may follow the cliff edge (not too closely!) to the north-northeast and pick up the Boutte du Cap Trail, which heads uphill toward two kittiwake colonies, including the largest kittiwake colony on the west coast of Newfoundland. Wooden posts with red painted tops indicate the way through stunted tuckamore forests and exposed barrens and along the 213-metre-high cliffs.

You'll know you've arrived at the first colony by the noise (and perhaps the smell, if you are

This trail offers a glimpse into the life of the Acadians who lived in this area in the nineteenth century. Boutte du Cap Park holds the only Acadian monument in Newfoundland. The traditional bread oven is for public use, and bread is baked in it during the summer.

downwind). Farther along the trail is a second kittiwake colony (at approximately 48.48444, -59.25257); the trail is not well-marked after this second colony, and GPS, map, and compass are recommended if venturing farther. Return by the same route.

Distance: 3-kilometre (6-kilometre return) linear trail.

Trailhead access: Take Route 460 to the Port au Port Peninsula. Stay left and drive to the community of Cape St. George, and turn into Boutte du Cap Park. Park by the bread oven or the interpretation panels at the end of the road: 48.4644273, -59.2628114.

Amenities: Benches, interpretation panels.

Keep in mind: Be extremely cautious during windy or foggy days; stay back from the cliff edge as cliffs may be undercut and unstable.

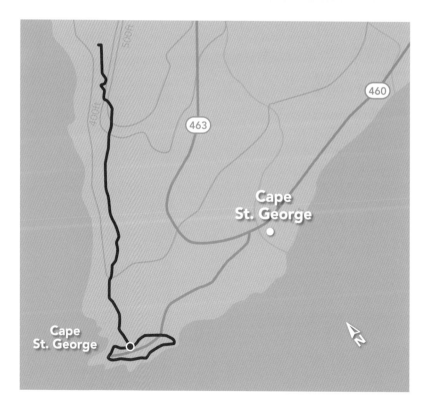

① Port au Port West

Beginning from the west end of the parking area, follow the trail along the coast as it winds between the stunted boreal forest and the limestone shoreline.

⭐ The limestone coast hosts many fossils from the Ordovician Period (443–485 million years ago), including trilobites, ammonites, and fossilized plants.

Hikers will be treated to a view of the Lewis Hills in the background, and unique eroded limestone designs in the foreground. The ocean in this area is remarkably clear: from most points on the trail you can see its bottom.

The Gravels Walking Trail is well-maintained, with stairs, wooden bridges, and small offshoot trails that lead to the sea or back toward the main road. Take the side trail to Aguathuna to visit Our Lady of Mercy church, one of Newfoundland's oldest and largest wooden buildings. The site also hosts a separate museum and tearoom. Guided tours are available.

Return to the Gravels Trail parking area by following the main road or returning along the trail.

Distance: 3.5-kilometre trail network.

Trailhead: From Stephenville take Route 460 to Port au Port West. Along the isthmus, Gravels Pond is on your left and the parking area on your right. The trail begins at the west end of the parking area: 48.559, -58.7287.

Amenities: Picnic tables, garbage cans, and benches along the trail; interpretation signs and picnic tables at trailhead.

Keep in mind: Be wary about getting too close to the ocean; waves are powerful and the water cold.

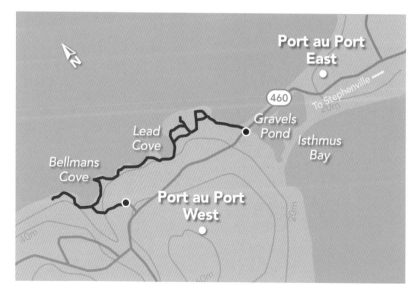

3 ## Noels Pond–Stephenville Crossing

The Indian Head Range Trail begins about 50 metres from the Noels Pond parking area. From the IATNL parking lot, walk left along a quad track until you see a sign for the trail on the right—once you're on it, it's easy to follow and well-marked.

> ⭐ Find the Indian Head, the rock formation from which the trail gets its name.

This section of the IATNL is rough and wet in places, with a few easy creek crossings. The trail passes mainly through forests, and terrain changes are fairly gradual with only a few short, steep rises to

access the barrens. From the 160-metre-high lookout, you can see Stephenville, Bay St. George, Port au Port, and the Lewis Hills.

The trail then leads you down toward Stephenville Crossing, ending at Seal Cove Road. Return by the same trail or arrange a shuttle back to the Noels Pond trailhead.

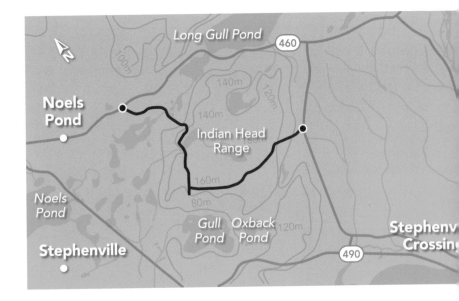

Distance: 7-kilometre (14-kilometre return) linear trail.

Trailhead access:
There are two trailheads:

■ From TCH, take Route 460. On your left, before the community of Noels Pond, is the IATNL parking lot: 48.5637, -58.498.

■ From TCH, take Route 490 to Stephenville Crossing. Take the last right into Stephenville Crossing, then the first left onto Seal Cove Road. The trailhead sign is about 1.5 kilometres in: 48.540059, -58.458977.

Amenities: None.

Keep in mind: Logs have been placed in wet sections to assist crossings. Be cautious: logs may be slippery or unstable.

Permits & fees: Donations toward trail upkeep are payable to IATNL.

Cold Brook–Serpentine Lake

*This is a backcountry route, **not** a maintained trail; most hikers take two to three days (one or two nights in a tent) to complete it. This description is from south to north.*

> ★ All three of Newfoundland's carnivorous plants are found in the Lewis Hills: butterwarts, pitcher plants, and sundews.

 Starting at the southern trailhead off Cold Brook Road, the Lewis Hills Trail crosses 2 kilometres of wetland, revealing spectacular views of a rust-coloured peridotite mountain range before descending to cross Fox Island River. After the river crossing, the trail rises again, through a peridotite valley with many waterfalls. This section brings hikers to a height of about 640 metres, before the final 4-kilometre ascent (174-metre elevation gain) to the Cabox, Newfoundland's highest point, at 814 metres.

From the Cabox, the route continues west across the hills to the rugged Molly Ann Gulch, a steep fjord-like valley with views of the Gulf of St. Lawrence. This excellent camping spot provides sheltered areas as well as prime sunset viewing.

From Molly Ann Gulch, continue north to Rope Cove Canyon and then cross the barrens, heading northeast toward Buds Lake overlooking the awe-inspiring Serpentine Valley. Be alert for caribou herds and moose.

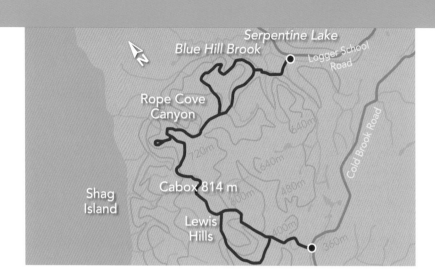

Descend Red Rocky Gulch, named for the peridotite rocks and boulders strewn along the valley floor. Along the descent, the route provides views of Serpentine Lake and the Blow Me Down Mountains before crossing Blue Hill Brook and connecting to Logger School Road at the northern trailhead.

Distance: 32-plus-kilometre linear route.

Trailhead access: A four-wheel drive with good clearance is needed to access trailheads; roads may be washed out and rough. Multiple logging roads may be confusing; IATNL back-country maps and GPS track are highly recommended.

■ Southern trailhead: 2.5 kilometres past Noels Pond, turn off Route 460 toward the community of Cold Brook. On your right, before the community, is a logging road and parking area. Drive approximately 25 kilometres along the logging road, following the few IATNL blazes.

■ Northern trailhead: Exit TCH approximately 10 kilometres west of Corner Brook onto Logger School Road. Follow it for about 17.5 kilometres, then take a right (you'll see Serpentine

Lake from this junction). Drive another 12.5 kilometres until you reach IATNL's trailhead sign.

Amenities: None.

Keep in mind: Navigation is essential throughout this trek. Take extra precautions during low cloud or fog situations. The weather, particularly the wind, along the coast can be extreme. This is not a marked route. A map, compass skills, and a government-issued topographic map are necessary. Do not rely solely on GPS.

Permits & fees: Donations toward trail upkeep are payable to IATNL.

Map #: 12B16 & 12B15

Note: This multi-day hike can be combined with Blow Me Down Mountain Trail (hike #16).

Barachois Provincial Park

The first section of Erin Mountain Trail travels over well-maintained boardwalks through boreal forest to a lower lookout. The trail from the lower lookout to the top of Erin Mountain climbs steadily through forest and, in some places, crosses over exposed rock, making the route to the summit more challenging.

The waters and forests of Barachois Pond have long been important to residents of St. George's Bay. Moose, caribou, and rabbit hunting provided fresh meat; white pine, fir, and spruce were used for house and boat construction and fuel. By 1958, commercial lumbering combined with blister rust disease had exhausted most of the white pine stands. Barachois Pond and surrounding area became a park in 1962.

Look for plagioclase and blue-green pyroxene crystals in the bedrock.

At the 340-metre summit, you'll be rewarded with a panoramic view of Bay St. George and the blue waters of the Gulf of St. Lawrence. Look behind you to see the top of the Long Range Mountains. The summit is a scenic picnic area; you may even be lucky enough to see moose near the ponds to the east.

Follow the same route back to the campground, but pause to enjoy the views. A beach and swimming area at Barachois Park is ideal for a refreshing post-hike dip.

Barachois
Pond

**Barachois
Provincial
Park**

Distance: 4-kilometre linear trail (8-kilometre return).

Trailhead access: Barachois Park entrance is on the TCH between the two exits for Stephenville. Pay at the check-in and drive to the end of the peninsula, where a small parking area marks the trailhead: 48.4811522, -58.2610044.

Amenities: Campsites and a day-use area with picnic tables, playground, drinking water, and toilets.

Keep in mind: Pace yourself—some sections of this trail rise steeply. Always look out for moose, caribou, and other large wildlife.

Permits & fees: $5 per vehicle daily permit fee or $20 seasonal permit.

BAY OF ISLANDS & HUMBER VALLEY

The trails in the Bay of Islands and Humber Valley rival those in Gros Morne National Park for their diversity of distances, terrain, and scenery. All of the Bay of Islands and Humber Valley trails listed below are used year-round by hikers, snowshoers, and cross-country skiers.

The Bay of Islands is steeped in history. The area was first charted by Captain James Cook. In his 1767 survey, Cook mapped the Port au Port Peninsula, the Port au Choix Peninsula, and also measured the depths of both St. George's Bay and the Bay of Islands. He also travelled 24 kilometres up the Humber River to map the nearby mountains and the river's depth. Cook's name appears twice on maps of the Bay of Islands, at Cooks Cove and Cooks Brook; he named places after his survey ships (the *Lark* in Lark Harbour, for example) and used English river names (Humber River). Visit Cook's Lookout in Corner Brook to learn more about this world traveller and his importance to Newfoundland.

Bay of Islands and the Humber Valley have been recognized as one of the best places in the province for adventure tourism, not only for hikers but also for sea kayakers, salmon fishers, hunters, downhill and cross-country skiers, and snowmobilers. Access to the trailheads is easy and the variety of landscapes, routes, and urban and remote areas will suit everyone's needs and interests.

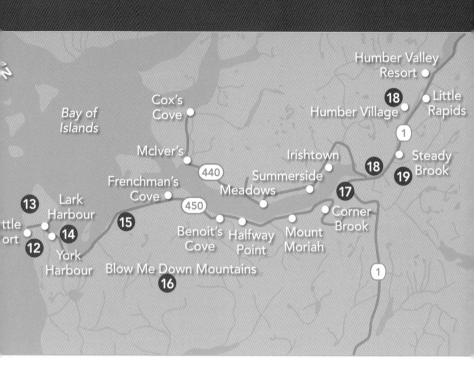

Trails of the Southwest Coast

12. Cedar Cove & Little Port Head Lighthouse Trails / Little Port
13. Bottle Cove & South Head Lighthouse Trails / Lark Harbour
14. Tortoise Mountain Trail / Lark Harbour (Blow Me Down Provincial Park)
15. Copper Mine to Cape Trail / York Harbour
16. Blow Me Down Mountain Trail / York Harbour
17. Corner Brook Stream Walking Trails / Corner Brook
18. Humber Valley Trail / Corner Brook, Humber Village, Humber Valley Resort
19. Marble Mountain & Steady Brook Falls Trails / Steady Brook

1 Cedar Cove Trail

Turning left onto the Cedar Cove Trail takes you along the base of Little Port Head and directly out to Cedar Cove Beach. The trail is well-maintained and -marked, with little elevation change. The beach is scattered with driftwood, and it's a favourite place for kite flying. Follow the trail back out to the parking area.

Outer Bay of Islands
Enhancement Committee

3 Little Port Head Lighthouse Trail

Little Port Head Lighthouse Trail heads toward the harbour. You'll begin to ascend immediately; the narrow trail has a steep drop-off on your right. At the modern light station, you'll have a view of the mouth of the Bay of Islands. Guernsey Island, the tallest island in the bay, is to the north-northwest. Continue to the 250-metre summit and traverse across the head to see the Lewis Hills to the south and Lark Harbour and Blow Me Down Mountains to the east. The descent is very steep and may be slippery, but ropes are available to assist you. At the trail junction, turn right to go to Cedar Cove Beach or left to return to the parking area.

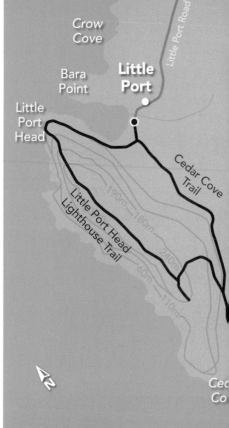

Crow Cove

Bara Point

Little Port

Little Port Head

Little Port Road

Cedar Cove Trail

Little Port Head Lighthouse Trail

190m — 180m — 210m — 60m — 170m

Cedar Cove

★ The Bay of Islands was originally mapped by Captain James Cook, between 1764 and 1767. York Harbour and Lark Harbour, two of the four communities that make up the Outer Bay of Islands (with Bottle Cove and Little Port), were named after Cook's ships HMS *York* and HMS *Lark*, which belonged to the Royal Navy's Newfoundland squadron. The first permanent settlers in the Outer Bay of Islands arrived early in the nineteenth century as the area developed its fishery and lumber industries.

Distances: 1.8-kilometre linear and 3-kilometre loop trail options.

Trailhead access: Take Route 450 toward Lark Harbour. Turn left after the gas station toward Little Port (on Little Port Road). Drive to the end of the road and park on the far left near the stairs. Ensure your vehicle is not obstructing traffic: 49.1019, -58.3644.

Amenities: None.

Keep in mind: The ascent and descent of Little Port Head are steep and can be slippery year-round. Use extreme caution along the trail, especially near cliff edges, as they may be undercut. Extremely high winds can make hiking challenging and potentially dangerous.

Permits & fees: Donations toward trail upkeep are payable to Outer Bay of Islands Enhancement Committee (OBIEC) via the towns of Lark Harbour or York Harbour.

1 Bottle Cove Trail

Bottle Cove Trail is a 1-kilometre network between Bottle Cove Beach and Miranda Cove that showcases

the beautiful coastline: steep cliffs, sea caves, and white sand beaches. Seals and whales often swim here—and so can you, during the warmer

months. A sea cave at the south end of Bottle Cove Beach is accessible at low tide. From the Bottle Cove parking lot, start hiking at the large trailhead sign.

3 Southhead Lighthouse Trail

Follow the signs from the Bottle Cove parking lot for the 3.3-kilometre Southhead Lighthouse Trail. The trail passes a communication station and heads toward the Murray Mountains. The first part of the trail meanders through forest and bog and leads into a valley. The next section is a steady climb up the valley. The 350-metre elevation gain is gratifying, however, as it brings you to a breathtaking view of Guernsey Island, the Bay of Islands, and the North Arm Hills (across the bay). The trail loops at the end, and hikers return via the same route.

Distances: 1-kilometre trail network and 3.3-kilometre linear trail (6.6-kilometre return) options.

Trailhead access: Follow Route 450 to Lark Harbour. Turn left after the gas station onto Little Port Road; when the road branches, stay right. Follow the gravel road and take the first left into the Bottle Cove parking area: 49.1167753, -58.4071169.

Amenities: None.

Keep in mind: As these trails follow high cliffs, stay back from the edges. Be aware of the tides when venturing to the sea cave.

Permits & fees: Donations toward trail upkeep are payable to OBIEC via the towns of Lark Harbour or York Harbour.

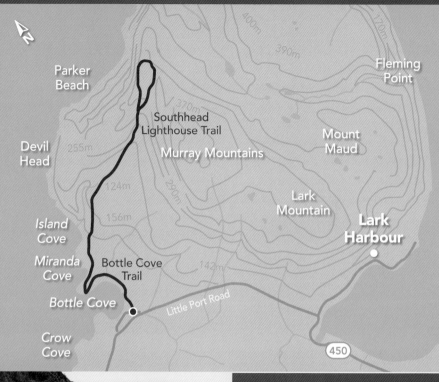

Parker
Beach

Southhead
Lighthouse Trail

Murray Mountains

Devil
Head

255m

124m

156m

*Island
Cove*

*Miranda
Cove*

Bottle Cove
Trail

Bottle Cove

142m

Little Port Road

*Crow
Cove*

450

390m

Fleming
Point

Mount
Maud

Lark
Mountain

**Lark
Harbour**

⭐ Southhead Lighthouse was
established on a stone cliff at
Southhead in 1925 to help ships
reach the Corner Brook pulp
and paper mill. It was built as a
square wooden structure topped
by an open wooden framework
that supported an acetylene gas
lantern. The dwelling at Southhead was intentionally burned in
1989, leaving just the octagonal
concrete tower; this was demol-
ished in 2010 and replaced with a
cylindrical, red-and-white-striped
fibreglass tower that supports a
solar-powered light. The lantern
room from the original octagonal tower is on display at the
trailhead.

③ Lark Harbour (Blow Me Down Provincial Park)

From the day-use parking lot at Blow Me Down Provincial Park, walk to the rocky beach and observe starfish, crabs, seabirds, and perhaps seals. The trail starts on the north end of the beach at the Governor's Staircase, which is built into the rocks and cliffside. Another trail access off the parking lot eliminates Governor's Staircase and the beach (take this trail if the staircase is inaccessible due to tides). The two trails meet before heading uphill.

> ★ The Governor's Staircase showcases the geology of 450-million-year-old rock. Look for quartz veins and interesting sedimentary rock formations.

A 250-metre steep climb brings hikers to a viewing platform overlooking the Blow Me Down Mountain Range and the Bay of Islands. From the platform, hikers can turn around or head to the tip

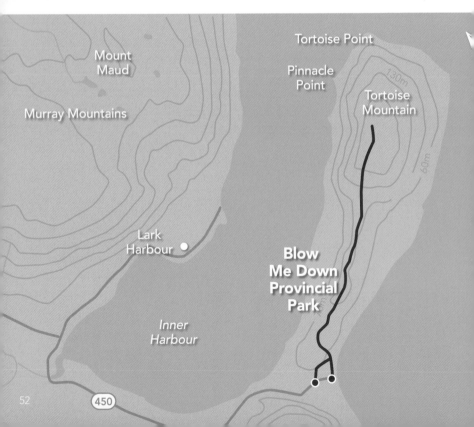

of the peninsula and the top of Tortoise Mountain, following the ridge through forest and across barrens.

On a clear day, the top of Tortoise Mountain offers a 360-degree view of the communities of Lark Harbour and York Harbour, as well as the Murray Mountains, Blow Me Down Mountains, and the Bay of Islands. Return by the same route.

Distance: 4.5-kilometre linear trail (9-kilometre return).

Trailhead access: Take Route 450 toward Lark Harbour and watch for Blow Me Down Provincial Park on your right: 49.090799, -58.3655517. The trail starts from either the day-use parking lot or its camping loop and the beach.

Amenities: Picnic tables and washrooms at campsite; picnic table at lookout platform.

Keep in mind: Governor's Staircase is inaccessible at high tides. The stairs on the trail's first section may be wet and slippery during heavy rains. No smoking is allowed on trails; all pets must be leashed.

Permits & fees: $5 per vehicle daily permit fee or $20 seasonal permit.

York Harbour

Remains from a copper mine can be seen near the parking area by the trailhead, giving this trail its name. The mine was founded in 1893 by Daniel Henderson, a prospector from Nova Scotia.

> ★ The view from the Blow Me Down peak may include caribou, moose, and other wildlife. In late summer, the blueberries found along the trail will be ripe for picking.

Outer Bay of Islands Enhancement Committee

Ascend a set of stairs, then follow a well-maintained trail. It's a steady climb to the Blow Me Down peak, but several lookouts and rest places are scattered along the way. Each lookout rewards hikers with a view of the Bay of Islands. The trail's first section climbs and meanders through dense forest. When it reaches the open barrens, there is an intersection for the backcountry trail (hike #16)—take the left trail toward the summit. Bogs and barrens change into subalpine landscape as you approach the 650-metre summit.

The view of Bay of Islands, Corner Brook, Lark Harbour, and other small communities is stunning, especially when the landscape is inflamed at sunrise or sunset.

Return to the parking area by the same route. From the parking area, another short trail leads to a waterfall, and is worth the detour. This trail is just off to the side, past the stairs to the main trail, at the end of the parking lot.

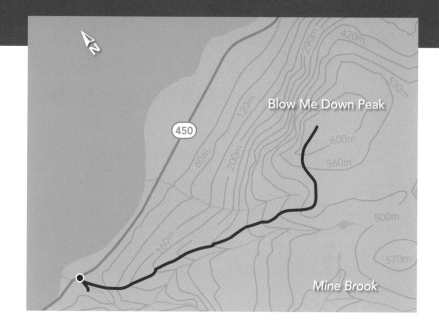

Blow Me Down Peak

Mine Brook

Distance: 3.8-kilometre linear trail (7.6-kilometre return).

Trailhead access: Follow Route 450 from Corner Brook. About 10 kilometres past Frenchman's Cove, on the left, an IATNL trail sign and a gravel road lead up to the parking area: 49.0625389, -58.3024524.

Amenities: Benches at parking area and along the trail.

Keep in mind: The trail's first section is steep, and muddy and slippery when it rains.

Permits & fees: Donations toward trail upkeep are payable to OBIEC via the towns of Lark Harbour or York Harbour.

York Harbour

*This is a backcountry route, **not** a maintained trail; most hikers take two to three days (one or two nights in a tent) to complete it.*

Starting from the northern trail-head, the first part of the trail is the same as that for the Copper Mine to Cape Trail (hike #15) and is well-marked.

Take the trail to the right at the fork in the open barrens, and trek 16 kilometres south across the mountaintop to arrive at Red Gulch. IATNL suggests a route

(shown on the map), but hikers can explore the mountain plateau. Must-sees are Red Gulch, with its orange-brown peridotite rocks; Simms Gulch, which is half peridotite and half slate grey; and Blow Me Down Gulch and its waterfall.

On the south side of the Blow Me Down plateau, Serpentine Lake and valley with the Lewis Hills as its backdrop are a remarkable sight. The trail wanders through marsh, bogs, forests, and rocky terrains. Be ready to bushwhack if exploring around the plateau.

Heading west from Red Gulch, the trail descends into the steep and meandering Simms Gulch until it reaches Serpentine Lake, where hikers must cross Serpentine River, to reach the Logger School Road trailhead access. This route requires a shuttle or arranged pickup and drop-off.

The peridotite mantle rock of Red Gulch was heaved up through plate tectonics and is the same as that of the Tablelands in Gros Morne National Park. It is part of the Bay of Islands ophiolite complex. This orange-brown rock has toxic amounts of heavy metals, making it difficult for most plants to survive—hence the Mars-like landscape.

The plateau meadows and bogs contain a rich diversity of wildflowers and plants. In late summer, blueberries are abundant and may attract black bears. This plateau is home to moose and herds of caribou.

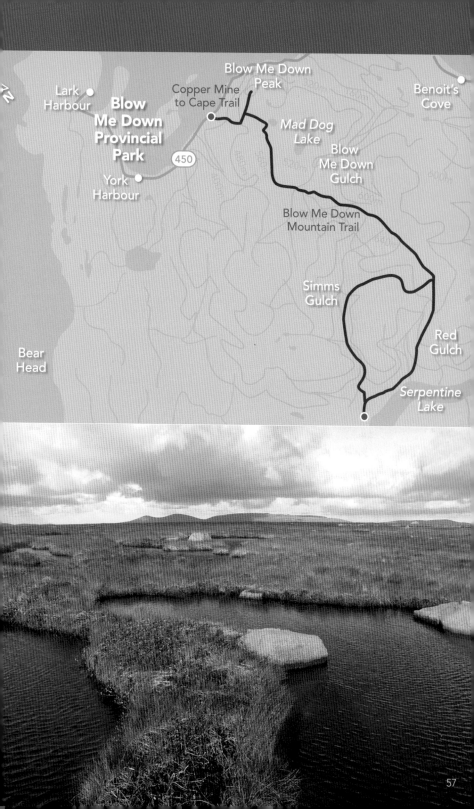

Lark
Harbour

**Blow
Me Down
Provincial
Park**

York
Harbour

450

Bear
Head

Copper Mine
to Cape Trail

Blow Me Down
Peak

Benoit's
Cove

Mad Dog
Lake

Blow
Me Down
Gulch

Blow Me Down
Mountain Trail

Simms
Gulch

Red
Gulch

Serpentine
Lake

Distance: 35+ kilometres.

Note: This hike can be combined with the Lewis Hills Trail (hike #10).

Trailhead access: A four-wheel drive with good clearance is strongly recommended; roads may be washed out and rough. The multiple logging roads can be confusing: accurate backcountry maps and a compass will be required for navigation. Contact IATNL for GPS reference points and route track.

■ Northern trailhead: Follow Route 450 from Corner Brook; about 10 kilometres past Frenchman's Cove is an IATNL trail sign on the left. An alternate trail access: Blow Me Down Nature Trail, 4 kilometres from Frenchman's Cove (this is a rougher, wetter access point, but the peridotite and gabbro valley is stunning).

■ Southern trailhead: Exit Route 1 onto Logger School Road, approximately 10 kilometres west of Corner Brook. Drive approximately 17 kilometres, turn right and head toward Serpentine Lake. Park at the end of the road. Walk to the west end of Serpentine Lake, cross the river and head toward Simms Gulch.

Amenities: None.

Keep in mind: This is a wilderness route. Do not rely solely on GPS, as the signal can be greatly reduced during cloudy days.

Corner Brook

The Corner Brook Stream Walking Trail network is made up of three main trails: Glynmill Inn Pond trail, Three Bear Mountain trail, and Corner Brook Gorge trail. Glynmill Inn Pond trail, the easiest and most accessible, consists of 2 kilometres of gravel walkways. During the summer, many events are held around the Glynmill Pond and in Margaret Bowater Park.

Three Bear Mountain trail has more elevation gain than the Glynmill Inn Pond trail but is only about 1 kilometre long. Side trails lead to views of the city; interpretation panels of Corner Brook's history and development are displayed along the trail.

Corner Brook Gorge trail is approximately 4 kilometres long and rated a moderate trail. It leads up to Corner Brook Gorge, where hikers can view the waterfalls and return via the same route or hike down to Crocker's Road. This trail meanders through the forest and along the wooden pipeline and crosses the Corner Brook stream.

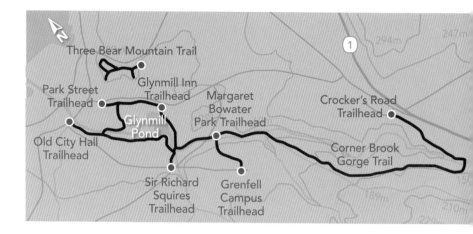

Distance: 7-kilometre trail network.

Trailhead access: The main entry area is at Margaret Bowater Park on O'Connell Drive: 48.9445528, -57.9351942. Other access points: Glynmill Inn, Park Street, Cobb Lane, Old City Hall (corner of Main St. and Mt. Bernard), Crocker's Road, and Sir Richard Squires Building; most have parking areas.

Amenities: Trails have rest spots, picnic areas, and lookouts. Margaret Bowater Park has multiple play-grounds, an unsupervised swimming area, canteen, and bathrooms.

Keep in mind: The swans in Glynmill Inn Pond, although used to visitors, can be dangerous if aggravated. Keep dogs leashed and clean up after your pet.

Permits & fees: Donations toward trail upkeep are payable to the Corner Brook Stream Development Corporation (CBSDC). Participation in the memorial program is appreciated.

Corner Brook

The Humber Valley Trail follows the hilltops along the north side of the Lower Humber River, from the southern trailhead near Ballam Bridge to Wild Cove Road to Humber Village and finally to the northernmost trailhead in Humber Valley Resort.

> This trail is in the Long Range Mountains and follows the Humber River from the Humber Arm estuary to Humber Valley Resort. This river is one of the world's best Atlantic salmon-fishing rivers.

For a half-day hike: summiting the Old Man in the Mountain is a 2.5-kilometre (5-kilometre return) section of the Humber Valley Trail. The trail quickly climbs about 300 metres to the top of the Long Range Mountains and follows the ridge along the north shore of the Humber River. At the second pond, follow the shoreline to the right until you see the trail again. The Old Man in the Mountain lookout affords a bird's-eye view of the Humber

River, Corner Brook, and Humber Arm. Return by the same route. This section is well-marked.

For a full-day or overnight hike: continue northeast on the trail from the Old Man in the Mountain lookout. Follow the ridge and descend onto Wild Cove Road. Head toward Wild Cove Lake, cross the rough bridge at the east end of the lake, then turn right to meet the trail again. This section, wet year-round, climbs to the next ridge. The trail offers panoramic views of the Humber Valley from Deer Lake to the Blow Me Down Mountains, with North Arm Hills to the west and Marble Mountain ski

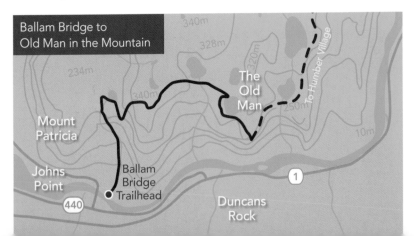

Ballam Bridge to Old Man in the Mountain

Old Man in the Mountain to Humber Village

hill to the south. The route intersects with a quad trail just above Humber Village. Follow it downhill until you reach a fence and a gravel road near a communication tower (48.9883230, -57.7703624).

To continue from the intersection at Humber Village, hike east along the ridge. The route veers inland toward Little North Pond, then back toward the Humber River until intersecting with a Humber Valley Resort service road (49.0229536, -57.6875365). Few signs or markers indicate the last two sections of the trail; navigation and route-finding skills are essential.

Distance: 25-kilometre linear trail.

Trailhead access: There are four trailheads for this trail. Contact IATNL for GPS reference points and route track.

■ Southern trailhead: From Route 1, take the exit for Corner Brook via Riverside Drive. Take the first right onto Route 440, cross Ballam Bridge, and immediately turn right on Riverside Extension / Bear Head Road. Follow the gravel road around to the left and turn left into the parking area: 48.9532917, -57.8860611.

■ Off Wild Cove Road, 6 kilometres past Ballam Bridge on Route 440. Drive to the end of the pond, turn left, and park on the right. The trail to go south (toward the Old Man in the Mountain) is directly off Wild Cove Road. To head north, cross the small bridge by the parking lot; the trail is on the right.

■ Enter Humber Village, take the first left and follow the main road to the communication tower. Park there. Go around the fence on the right-hand side and hike up the old quad trail to IATNL junction.

■ Northern trailhead (Humber Valley Resort): Take Exit 11 from Route 1 and follow the signs into Humber Valley resort. Drive straight on the main road, past the golf clubhouse, here the road becomes gravel. Take the first road on the left. Park at the pumphouse or, if driving a four-by-four, continue up the road and park near IATNL's trail sign.

Amenities: None.

Keep in mind: This is a moose (September–February) and small game (year-round) hunting area. Wear orange in the fall, and hikers, with dogs off leash, should be cautious. The Humber Village to Humber Valley section is not well-marked; be prepared with map and compass.

Permits & fees: Donations toward trail upkeep are payable to IATNL.

Map #: 12A13, 12H4

Humber Village to
Humber Valley Resort

Marble Mountain Trail

Follow the gravel access road and either take the Steady Brook trail or stay on this road and climb gradually. Both trails merge at the chlorine treatment hut. Continue straight on the gravel road until the road forks. Take the right road, go around the gate, and keep climbing the road past the two ski lifts and up to the Doppler weather station—a white tower with a big ball on top—at about 550 metres.

At the top of Marble Mountain is a panoramic view of the Bay of Islands, Corner Brook, Blow Me Down Mountains, North Arm Hills, Humber Valley, and Steady Brook. If you can, hike to the summit just before sunset and watch as the sun sets over the horizon of the Gulf of St. Lawrence. Start your return just after sunset to make it back before dark. Bring a flashlight! Descend along the same route.

> ★ The road to the Doppler weather station is a winter ski run called Country Road; it is accessible to hikers only outside the skiing season. The climb up "Marble" Mountain actually brings you to the summit of Musgrave Mountain.

Steady Brook Falls Trail

From the parking area, start up the gravel access road, turn left and cross the little bridge and follow the signs for Steady Brook Falls. The first section leads up to stairs and a wooden lookout platform. Continuing up the stairs will take you up the trail along the edge of Steady Brook Gorge to the top of the waterfall. Return by the same route.

Distance: 3-kilometre linear trail (6-kilometre return).

Trailhead access: Exit Route 1 into Steady Brook and follow the road behind Tim Horton's. Before the bridge, turn right into a gravel parking area: 48.94978, -57.8235719. The road up the hill is the trail.

Amenities: None on the trail; Tim Horton's, gas station, and other stores near the trailhead.

Keep in mind: This trail is located on a ski hill. Be courteous to other users and respect directions given by ski hill personnel. Dogs can be off leash.

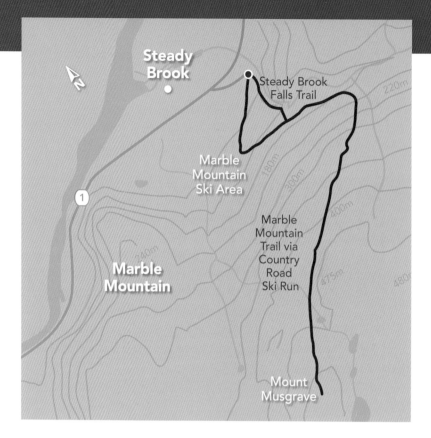

Steady
Brook

Steady Brook
Falls Trail

220m

Marble
Mountain
Ski Area

180m

300m

1

400m

Marble
Mountain
Trail via
Country
Road
Ski Run

**Marble
Mountain**

440m

475m

480m

Mount
Musgrave

GROS MORNE NATIONAL PARK

It's no surprise that Gros Morne National Park, designated a UNESCO World Heritage Site in 1987 for its geological history and natural beauty, contains some of the most majestic scenery in Canada.

See for yourself, as you hike the wide variety of trails throughout the park. Explore the glacially carved valleys, ancient mountaintops, coastal flatlands, and unearthly Tablelands (used as a Mars analogue by NASA researchers). Each trail offers something special, from geological wonders to wildlife sightings and towering waterfalls, and always a story to tell. Come here for a fully illustrated guide to plate tectonics or to see the earth's mantle—exposed. Welcome to some of the best hiking in western Newfoundland!

Trails of Gros Morne National Park

20. Overfalls Trail / Trout River
21. Trout River Pond Trail / Trout River
22. Green Gardens Trails / Route 431
23. Tablelands Trail / Route 431
24. Lookout Trail / Woody Point
25. Stanleyville Trail / Lomond
26. Lomond River Trail / Lomond
27. Stuckless Pond Trail / Lomond
28. James Callaghan Trail (Gros Morne Mountain) / Route 430
29. Baker's Brook Falls Trail / Route 430
30. Green Point Coastal Trail / Route 430
31. Western Brook Pond & Snug Harbour Trails / Route 430
32. Long Range Traverse / Route 430
33. North Rim Traverse / Route 430
34. Cow Head Lighthouse Trail / Cow Head

Permits & fees

■ All trails require a park pass. Daily and annual passes can be purchased at the Discovery Centre in Woody Point, the information kiosk off Route 430 before Wiltondale, or at the visitor centre at the Norris Point turnoff.

■ Extra fees apply for the use of backcountry trails and campsites.

■ Some trails require boat access; extra fees apply.

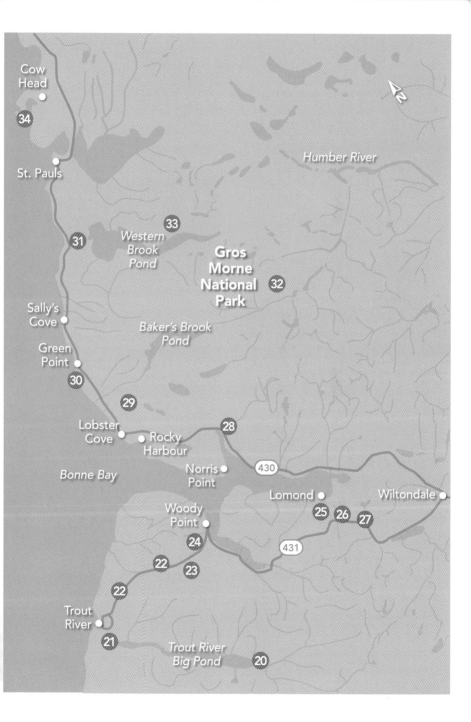

Trout River

To reach the Overfalls Trail, you must take a boat shuttle from Trout River to the eastern end of Trout River Pond. The boat trip is about one hour and travels along the south edge of the Tablelands, providing an excellent opportunity to view this favourite destination of geologists.

 Walk southwest on the beach, away from the Tablelands, until you see a trail, signs, or flagging tape leading into the forest. Follow the dry, even trail along the west branch of Trout River. The trail climbs from sea level to about 200 metres by the Overfalls. About midway, there is a side loop that you can climb to a lookout that provides views of Trout River Pond valley, the Tablelands, and the Overfalls.

The main trail does not lead to the base of the Overfalls but instead traverses the rim of the small valley created by the Overfalls waterfall, and is still quite rough. As of 2014, the trail to the top of the falls is incomplete, but it is worth the trek to where the trail ends to have a better view of the falls. Return the way you came, meeting your return shuttle at the beach. Watch for caribou and moose— both are commonly encountered along this trail.

> ★ The Overfalls Trail is the first IATNL-Gros Morne National Park partnership trail, established in 2011. It will eventually provide access to the North Arm hills and more IATNL trails.

Distance: 5-kilometre (10-kilometre return) linear trail.

Trailhead access: Take Route 431 to Trout River. At the stop sign, turn left onto Main Street. Follow Main Street (stay left) until the parking area: 49.1061, -58.1267. The trailhead is accessed via boat shuttle. Contact IATNL for shuttle options.

Amenities: None.

Keep in mind: This new trail may be quite rough in sections. Arrange a boat shuttle for a round-trip. Some stream crossings are challenging early in the season or after heavy rains.

Trout
River
Big Pond

Trout River

Overfalls

3 Trout River

Trout River Pond Trail is well signed, with a kilometre marker about every 500 metres or so. The first 3.5 kilometres has little elevation change as it travels through the forest with occasional scattered views of Trout River Pond. The scenery gradually transitions to smaller trees and tuckamore.

Eventually the trail brings you to exposed barrens covered by orange peridotite and serpentine rocks. You'll have to make a few small stream crossings, but these are easily done by hopping from rock to rock. The trail provides access to rocky beaches along the way.

Within the final 3 kilometres of trail, you'll climb to an elevation of about 110 metres. Enjoy the lookout where Trout River Pond narrows before it opens up again. Continue hiking to the second lookout—red Adirondack chairs await you. Sit and appreciate the scenery of the Tablelands and the cliffs surrounding the pond.

Return to the parking area the way you came.

> ★ This trail takes you along the edge of the Tablelands and up the glacial valley of Trout River Pond.

Distance: 7-kilometre linear trail (14-kilometre return).

Trailhead access: Take Route 431 to Trout River. Turn left onto Main Street and follow the signs for the trail (not the campground). The trail starts at the parking lot: 49.4607471, -58.1164384.

Amenities: Picnic tables, washrooms, a shelter, a playground, and a dock at the parking area; halfway along the trail is an outhouse.

Keep in mind: Some parts of the trail may be muddy and slippery. Stream crossings may be challenging after the snow melts; during summer, crossings are easier.

Route 431

You may hike Green Gardens several ways: short routes are linear trails to the coast and back; long routes lead to the ocean, follow the coastline, and loop back to the start.

Green Gardens via Long Pond short route is the most popular. Begin at the Long Pond parking area and head across a barren landscape of frost-cracked, orange-brown peridotite boulders. The trail rises to a viewpoint, where the rock type changes and the forest begins. Turn left at the junction and descend through forest to the coast. The trail ends in a staircase leading down to a beach beside a cliff of pillow lava. Return by the same route. The return is entirely uphill and steep in places.

Wallace Brook short route, 3 kilometres longer than the Long Pond route to the coast, begins at the Wallace Brook parking area. Cross a

small suspended bridge and follow the stairs down toward Wallace Brook. Two river crossings are required before you arrive at a beautiful beach and a stunning landscape of pillow lava formations. Return by the same route: uphill most of the way and steep in places.

To hike the Green Gardens long route, leave from either trailhead and complete a coastal loop to return to the starting point.

★ The rugged coastline is a geologist's paradise of volcanic formations. These eruptions occurred over 600 million years ago when the continents were splitting and oceans forming.

Watch for a sea cave, accessible during low tide, along the Long Pond to Green Gardens short route.

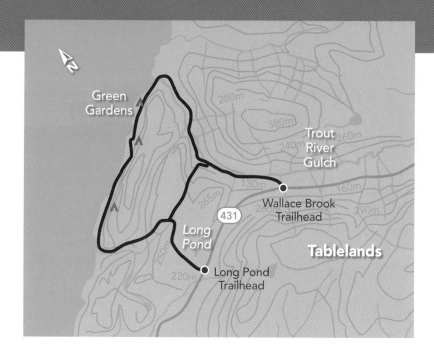

Green
Gardens

280m

380m

260m

Trout
River
Gulch

240m

130m

160m

190m

Wallace Brook
Trailhead

431

Tablelands

Long
Pond

265m

250m

220m

Long Pond
Trailhead

Distances: Via Long Pond: short route 4.5-kilometre linear trail (9-kilometre return); long route 14.5-kilometre loop.

Via Wallace Brook: short route: 6-kilometre linear trail (12-kilometre return); long route: 16-kilometre loop.

Trailhead access: Trailheads are on Route 431 between Woody Point and Trout River:

■ Wallace Brook trailhead: 11 kilometres from Woody Point (5 kilometres from Trout River): 49.4952560, -58.0395673.

■ Long Pond trailhead: 13 kilometres from Woody Point (3 kilometres from Trout River): 49.4913366, -58.0746785.

Amenities: Outhouses in parking areas and at the coast; tent platforms provided.

Keep in mind: Wallace Brook water level may be high during the spring or after a heavy rain; extra footwear (ideally water shoes) is recommended. Stay back from cliff edges as some places may be undercut; stay on the trails.

Route 431

As you drive to the Tablelands trailhead, notice how the road separates the orange, barren terrain of the Tablelands to the south from the lush green hills to the north. The valley floor is an ancient fault line; to the north are metamorphosed gabbro and other types of oceanic crust, while to the south is the ophiolite complex known as the Tablelands.

The first part of the trail crosses the broad, barren valley of Trout River Gulch and is strewn with peridotite rocks, moved by the glaciers that covered this region more than 10,000 years ago. These orange-brown cliffs tell the story of plate tectonics; the landscape depicts a time when the North American and African plates collided. The complex originated tens of kilometres below the earth's surface, in the upper mantle. Geologists from all over the world come to see this prime example of exposed mantle. This trail provides an up-close and intimate experience with this weird and wonderful geological feature.

The trail leads to a viewing platform beside Winterhouse Brook in

During the summer, guided hikes with National Park interpreters are offered; these are highly recommended.

Some wildflowers grow amongst this unique geology but, due to high levels of iron and magnesium, nothing else grows here.

Distance: 2-kilometre linear trail (4-kilometre return).

Trailhead access: Follow Route 431 toward Trout River. The parking area and trailhead are on the left, about 4.5 kilometres past the Discovery Centre: 49.4782798, -57.9738196.

Amenities: Outhouse and garbage bins in parking lot.

Keep in mind: The snow melts slowly on the north face of the Tablelands and may cover parts of the trail early in the season.

the centre of the majestic Winter House Gorge. This is an easy trail along a well-maintained gravel walkway with little elevation gain. Return along the same route.

Shoal
Brook

431

176m

176m

360m

337m

250m

270m

Tablelands

*Winterhouse
Brook*

489m

570m

650m

490m

Woody Point

This often-overlooked trail grants hikers access to one of the greatest views of Gros Morne National Park. From the Discovery Centre trailhead, you'll quickly climb 350 metres through boreal forest to reach the barren, boggy summit and the lookout. The first section is linear, but the trail then splits into a loop that goes around the top of Partridge Berry Hill. Stay to the right to reach the viewing platform more quickly.

From the platform, the stunning landscape of Bonne Bay, the Tablelands, and Gros Morne Mountain can be appreciated. Whales and icebergs may be sighted during appropriate times of the year. Continue on to complete the loop of Partridge Berry Hill, or return the way you came.

Distance: 5-kilometre loop.

Trailhead access: Follow Route 431 toward Woody Point, turn left toward Trout River. Turn right at the Discovery Centre and park: 49.4944532, -57.9241429. The trailhead is well signed.

Amenities: Washrooms, phones, and park information at the Discovery Centre; benches and chairs at the lookout.

Keep in mind: Parts of the trail may be muddy during periods of heavy rain in early spring and late fall. Extreme winds may be experienced on the exposed summit.

★ The landscape of this trail is a complete contrast to the landscape of the Tablelands. Well vegetated, the trail travels over metamorphosed gabbro and other types of oceanic crust, which contains the required elements for plant life. The summit provides a perfect habitat for pitcher plants, Newfoundland and Labrador's provincial flower and one of three carnivorous plants found in the province.

An exceptional hike to start a journey through Gros Morne National Park, it offers a bird's-eye view of all the major park features and helps you get your bearings. However, if you are hiking on a foggy or cloudy day, remember that visibility may be reduced.

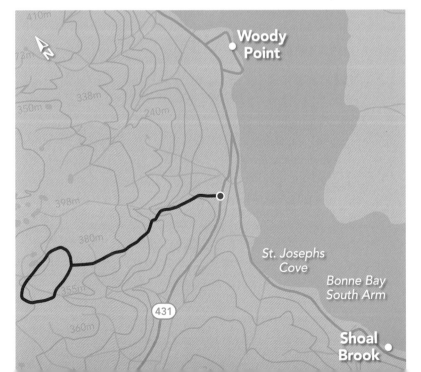

Lomond

Stanleyville Trail starts with a gradual ascent and a few bridges over small streams. Next, a steeper section with stairs leads to the highest point, about 110 metres. From this summit, look back toward Lomond and the east arm of Bonne Bay—a gorgeous landscape of hills and cliffs—before descending to the beach of Paynes Cove and Stanleyville.

From the beach you may see whales, seals, and seabirds. Stanleyville has been deserted for over 80 years and it's a lovely place to explore—garden plants and logging machinery are visible reminders of settlement. When you're ready, turn around and return the way you came. Watch for moose along the trail.

In the early 1900s, logging was a major industry and white pine the main source of lumber. In 1899, the McKie brothers built a sawmill in Stanleyville and from this started commercial lumbering. The site was abandoned in the 1920s when the St. Lawrence Timber, Pulp, and Steamship Company set up a larger operation in Lomond Cove, where this trail begins. Look for remnants of this abandoned community along the shoreline.

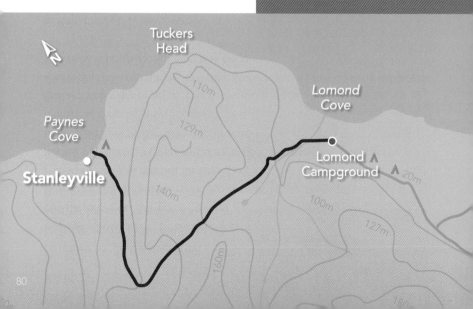

Tuckers Head

Lomond Cove

Paynes Cove

Lomond Campground

Stanleyville

Distance: 2-kilometre linear trail (4-kilometre return).

Trailhead access: On Route 431, 16 kilometres from Wiltondale, turn right and follow signs for Lomond Campground: 49.4591664, -57.7599048. The trailhead is at the end of the campground parking lot behind two brown buildings.

Amenities: Washrooms, showers, picnic tables, and a shelter at the trailhead; at Stanleyville beach, an outhouse, picnic table, chairs, and a primitive campsite.

Keep in mind: Many moose live in this area. Use extreme caution if encountering a cow with calf in the spring or a male in the fall mating season. Be careful in steep sections as the trail may be muddy and slippery during rainy periods.

Lomond

Distance: 6-kilometre linear trail (12-kilometre return).

Trailhead access: There are two trailheads:

■ From Wiltondale, follow Route 431 for about 16 kilometres until you see the trailhead sign and parking area on your right: 49.4268104, -57.7390852.

■ The second trailhead is on the access road for Lomond Campground and is marked with a trail map: 49.4506875, -57.7548265.

Amenities: Outhouse and garbage bins in the Lomond / Stuckless Pond parking lot.

Keep in mind: Some sections of the trail become muddy and slippery. Be aware of tidal changes.

Lomond River Trail meanders along the Lomond River, with about 60 metres of elevation change, out to the estuary of the east arm of Bonne Bay.

From the parking lot, follow the signs and boardwalk down to the trail and turn left. The trail wanders through a mature forest and leads down to the Lomond River, crossing a few bridges and offering access to rock and sand beaches along the way. The tides from Bonne Bay affect the river's water level; if you explore the beaches, be vigilant about the tides or you may become trapped.

The meeting of Lomond River and the east arm of Bonne Bay creates an estuary full of diverse aquatic life. This region is home to many species of birds and in the fall ducks rest here during their migration south. The Lomond River is also an Atlantic salmon and sea-run trout route during the summer.

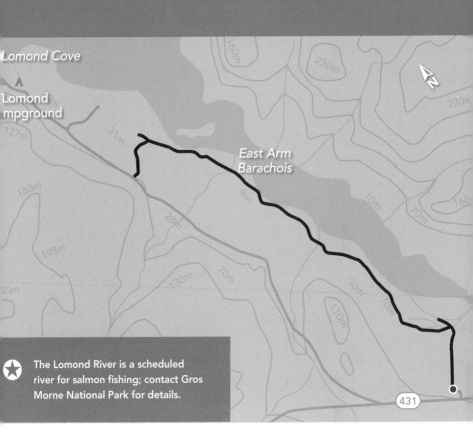

Lomond Cove

Lomond
mpground

East Arm
Barachois

127m
31m
180m
198m
10m
28th
9m
130m
70m
160m
230m
230m
10m
70m
160
30m
110m
431

⭐ The Lomond River is a scheduled river for salmon fishing; contact Gros Morne National Park for details.

Hike to the Lomond Campground access road trailhead. Return by the same trail or follow the access road to Route 431, turn left and walk along Route 431 to the parking area. This trail also connects with the Stuckless Pond Trail (hike #27).

Lomond

Leave the trailhead parking area and take the boardwalk down to the trail. Follow the signs for Stuckless Pond and veer to the right.

Descend a short downhill section and cross the Lomond River on a suspension bridge. This trail is a loop around Stuckless Pond; when the trail forks, go either right or left. The trail rolls up and down, with the highest point at an elevation of about 125 metres.

The pond can be accessed for a swim at a few locations. Birch stands, meadows, beaver dams, and the serenity of the area make this an enjoyable and relaxing hike. When you return to the fork, head back toward the Lomond River Bridge and the parking lot.

Most of this trail is located within the forest, making for good opportunities to see moose or other animals—you may encounter a moose grazing in a meadow or see a beaver at work.

Distance: 10-kilometre loop.

Trailhead access: From Wilton-dale, follow Route 431 for about 16 kilometres. The well-signed parking area is on the right: 49.4268104, -57.7390852.

Amenities: Outhouse and garbage bins at the main trailhead.

Keep in mind: This is a shared-use trail for bikers and hikers.

⭐ **This trail is an excellent intermediate cross-country biking route, with mixed terrain.**

Stuckless
Pond

Lomond River

230m
170m
150m
124m
150m
150m
80m
140m
70m
70m

128m

198m

240m

221m

240m

431

Route 430

Gros Morne means "Big Lone" in French. The mountain was given its name because it stands higher than the surrounding hills and is often hidden in the clouds. The trail is named after former United Kingdom Prime Minister James Callaghan (1976–79) for his conservation efforts.

From the parking lot, the trail climbs steadily to the base of Gros Morne Mountain. At about 300-metre elevation is a platform, an outhouse, and information signs; it makes a suitable rest spot.

The next section brings you to the gully, the steepest and hardest part of this trail; many of the rocks are loose. At the trail intersection keep going straight up the gully. It is safer for all hikers to hike the mountain loop clockwise.

At the top of the gully, the trail crosses the summit of 806 metres and then follows the edge of Ten Mile Gulch. As the trail descends, it wraps around the mountain to Ferry Gulch. The trail passes a small pond, where there are outhouses, picnic tables, and a backcountry campsite; if flies are abundant, keep moving! Follow the trail until it merges with the gully access trail. Return to the platform and continue to the parking lot.

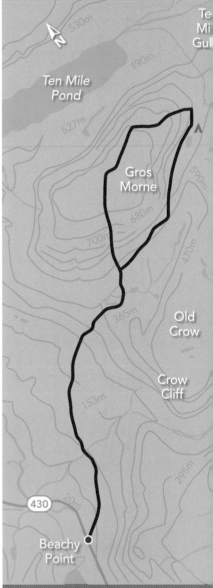

Gros Morne's summit is 806 metres, making it the second-highest mountain on the island of Newfoundland. The Cabox, in the Lewis Hills, is the tallest, at 814 metres. The mountain is home to caribou, moose, Arctic hare, and rock ptarmigan.

Distance: 16-kilometre loop.

Trailhead access: Trailhead is off Route 430, about 3 kilometres south of the Gros Morne visitor centre: 49.5653697, -57.8325148.

Amenities: Outhouses in the parking area, at the platform, and at the backcountry campsite; tent platforms and picnic tables at the backcountry campsite.

Keep in mind: It is easy to become disoriented when the fog rolls in, and this summit is exposed to high winds, lightning, and other extreme conditions. Heed all weather warnings.

Gros Morne Mountain is not open to hikers until July 1 in order to protect wildlife during critical weeks of reproduction and growth. No dogs allowed on this trail.

Pack out your garbage; do not remove anything (rocks, fossils, plants), and stay on the trail.

Route 430

From the parking lot of Berry Hill Campground, follow the trail along boardwalks and footpaths through a mix of forest, meadow, and boggy wetlands. This easy stroll takes you to Baker's Brook and the waterfall, Baker's Brook Overfalls.

Moose, squirrels, and grey jays are the most common wildlife along the trail but, if you're interested in local botany, the bogs and meadows boast a wide array of wildflowers.

Most of the trail has little elevation change, but at the end, you descend 30 to 40 metres with the help of stairs to see the falls up close. The falls are stunning and worth the hike—the brook runs over a series of ledges, creating a cascade effect.

Distance: 5-kilometre linear trail (10-kilometre return).

Trailhead access: Turn off Route 430 at Berry Hill Campground: 49.6250013, -57.927896. Pay fees at the gate and then drive straight, following the signs to the trailhead; the parking area is on the left.

Amenities: Washrooms, showers, picnic tables, a shelter, and campsites at Berry Hill Campground.

Keep in mind: Baker's Brook has a strong current and the water is cold; keep a close eye on small children near the water.

During the winter, this is an excellent snowshoeing and cross-country ski trail.

Route 430

This trail is part of the old Winter Mail Road that continues up to the Northern Peninsula. Before the road was cleared, dog teams hauled mail along this route, stopping at every community along the way.

> Green Point displays a 30-million-year record of deep ocean sediments in the exposed layers of shale. Gros Morne National Park offers a guided walk called "Stroll through Strata," in which park interpreters share the details of this exceptional geological site.

Beginning at Green Point Campground, the trail follows the coastline south, with little elevation change, crossing rocky shoreline, tuckamore forests, marshy ponds, and a traditional lobster cage. It offers fantastic views of the coastline; Green Gardens with its interesting rock formations can also be seen. Watch brilliant sunsets from the trail, and use your binoculars

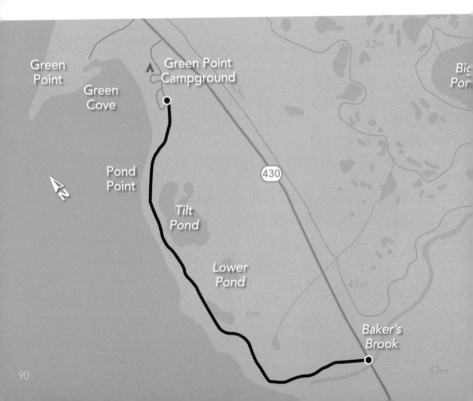

for sightings of migrating whales, ducks, and seabirds.

In 2000, Green Point was designated a Global Stratotype Section and Point (GSSP) and represents the division between Cambrian and the Ordovician periods (542–443 million years ago). In these limestone layers geologists found the first *Iapetognathus fluctivagus*, a conodont fossil that lies 4.8 metres below the earliest known planktic graptolite fossil.

Walk as far as you like and return along the coastline.

Distance: 3-kilometre linear trail (6-kilometre return).

Trailhead access: There are two trailheads on Route 430:

■ Green Point Campground: 49.6793501, -57.9574785.

■ The parking area at Baker's Brook Bridge: 49.8292314, -57.8560289. Signs indicate the trail.

Amenities: Picnic tables, outhouses, a shelter, and campsites at the campground.

Keep in mind: Most of the trail is exposed to the ocean and wind. Be aware of tidal changes.

Route 430

For both trails, follow the well-maintained trail and boardwalks toward Western Brook Pond.

1 Western Brook Pond Trail

Follow the Western Brook Pond trail; this is the same way you access the boat tour. When you reach a fork, keep right and head toward the dock. Enjoy a drink and a snack at the concession and savour the view of the landlocked fjord with its sheer 700-metre-high cliffs. Return along the same route.

Snug Harbour Trail

If you're hiking to Snug Harbour, keep left at the fork to go straight to your destination or go right and stop at the dock. From the dock, take the trail back out but stay to the right. The trails merge just before you wade across Western Brook. The Snug Harbour trail leads across Western Brook to a backcountry campsite at the foot of the Long Range Mountains. A rope across the brook assists with crossing. Return by the same route.

Distance: Western Brook Pond, 3-kilometre linear trail (6-kilometre return); Snug Harbour: 8-kilometre linear trail (16-kilometre return).

Note: These trails provide access to Long Range Traverse (hike #32) and North Rim Traverse (hike #33).

Trailhead access: Follow Route 430 approximately 28 kilometres past the visitor centre to the large parking area for Western Brook Pond: 49.7882564, -57.870836.

Amenities: Outhouses, benches, and interpretation panels along the trail. Washrooms and a small canteen at the dock.

Keep in mind: If you're doing the Snug Harbour Trail, be prepared to ford Western Brook; the water may be deep in the spring or after a heavy rainfall. Bring extra footwear (sandals or water shoes) for crossings.

Western Brook Pond, a freshwater pond, was once connected to the ocean, making it a true fjord. When the glaciers receded, the boggy lowlands rebounded, breaking off the fjord from the ocean. The cliffs and waterfalls along the pond are spectacular and the boat tour is well worth the ticket price.

Sandy Pond

Rocky Pond

30m

81m

121m

Snug Harbour

430

Western Brook Pond

35m

Lewis Pond

Western Brook Hill

93

Route 430

*This description is based on boating in via Western Brook Pond (northern trailhead, see hike #31) and hiking out at Gros Morne Mountain (southern trailhead, see hike #28). This is a backcountry route, **not** a maintained trail; most hikers take three to five days (two to four nights in a tent) to complete it.*

This multi-day hike starts with an easy 3 kilometres of gravel and boardwalk to the docks, from which you'll take the tour boat across Western Brook Pond. Bring your backcountry permit and transceiver. You'll be dropped off at the far end of the pond on a small dock in the shadow of steep cliffs.

The next section is challenging: you'll hike up and out of the fjord through meadows and forest, gaining approximately 500 metres. Follow the stream and stay to the right of the waterfall. Don't forget to stop and look behind you. The view of the fjord is impressive.

From the top of the fjord, head south toward Little Island Pond campsite (coordinates on Gros Morne website). Be prepared to bushwhack, cross streams and bogs, and deal with bugs. You'll encounter ponds of all sizes during your hike, so follow your map. As you continue south, use Marks Pond campsite, Harding's Pond campsite, Green Island Pond campsite, and Ferry Gulch as waypoints. Watch for caribou herds, moose, and ptarmigan and a diversity of flora, from bogs to barrens.

Eventually you'll see the rounded shape of Gros Morne Mountain, 806 metres high, as you pass Baker's Brook Gulch, and traverse the edge of Ten Mile Gulch. An array of great views of Bonne Bay, Rocky Harbour, the Tablelands, Ten Mile Pond, and many other communities reward you. Head down Ferry Gulch to the Gros Morne back-country campsite—this section is very steep!

From the campsite, you'll be on a marked trail. Either hike to the summit of Gros Morne Mountain or walk out Ferry Gulch toward the parking area. Take your transceiver back to the visitor centre.

Distance: 35-kilometre linear route.

Note: Long Range Traverse can be combined with North Rim Traverse (hike #33).

Trailhead access: Two trailheads, both on Route 430.

■ Northern trailhead: parking lot for Western Brook Pond, approximately 28 kilometres past the visitor centre: 49.7882564, -57.870836.

■ Southern trailhead: Gros Morne Mountain trailhead: 49.5653697, -57.8325148.

Amenities: Outhouses and picnic tables at the parking area; washrooms and concessions at the Western Brook Pond dock. Some backcountry campsites have wooden platforms, pit toilets, and food lockers or bear poles.

Keep in mind:

■ This is not a marked trail. Do not rely solely on GPS. You must have map and compass skills and a topographic map.

■ Visibility may be greatly reduced when the fog rolls in, forcing you to stop hiking to wait it out.

■ You'll receive a transceiver from the park, which must be returned at the end of your hike. Bring an emergency communication device: a marine radio, satellite phone, or SPOT. Cell phones do not work.

■ Cook and store food away from camp to discourage black bears.

■ Campfires are not permitted.

■ Don't be fooled: Herds of caribou and moose make paths all over the mountains. Stick to your map route.

Permits & fees

■ Hiking dates must be booked in advance. This is a popular route, and only nine people per campsite per night are allowed.

■ Arrive at least one day before your departure to attend a mandatory pre-trip planning session, which includes a map and compass skills assessment.

■ Reservation and backcountry camping fees apply.

■ When booking your hiking dates, book boat tickets as well (see information at the back of this book).

Map #: 12 H/12

Western Brook
Pond Trail

Western Brook
Pond

Baker's
Brook
Middle
Pond

Sally's
Cove

Baker's
Brook
Pond

650m

640m

Gros Morne
Mountain

Two Mile
Pond

430

Lobster
Cove

Rocky
Harbour

James
Callaghan
Trail

Pissing Mare Falls, which you'll see on the Western Brook Pond boat tour, is the highest waterfall in eastern North America, at 350 metres.

This hike takes place in the Long Range Mountains, a subsection of the Appalachian Mountain Range, making the traverse part of IATNL.

Route 430

*This description is based on hiking in at Snug Harbour and boating out at Western Brook Pond (see hike #32). This is a backcountry route, **not** a maintained trail; most hikers take three to five days (two to four nights in a tent) to complete it.*

Start your hike along the well-maintained Western Brook Pond trail. At the fork, stay left and continue toward Snug Harbour. Ford Western Brook to reach Snug Harbour campsite, which has a meadow for tents, a food hang, and an outdoor toilet. A beach on Western Brook Pond offers views of the cliffs.

> ⭐ This trail follows the cliff edge of the landlocked fjord of Western Brook. Watch for caribou herds, rock ptarmigan, and moose.

From Snug Harbour, walk to the end of the beach to a trail sign, and make your way uphill. There are two routes up to the North Rim: the right branch is steep and leads to a barren scrubby area; the left, more gradual, leads to a boggy meadow. Both branches rejoin the main trail and continue up onto the North Rim. An optional side trail leads to a lookout—the view is worth it!

A campsite is available at Long Pond and, next, beside a small pond (about six hours from Western Brook Pond, see GPS coordinates on Gros Morne website). There are no facilities at this site.

Continue toward the back of Western Brook fjord. Follow the brook that feeds into Western Brook fjord, keeping to the south side. Coming down into the fjord is very steep: stay left of the waterfall. After the waterfall, follow the brook to the campsite at the dock. Be ready at the appropriate time for boat pickup. Hike out to the parking area from the dock.

Snug
Harbour

430

Western Brook
Pond

Distance: 27-kilometre linear trail.

Note: North Rim Traverse can be combined with Long Range Traverse (hike #32). North Rim is less travelled and said to be more challenging than Long Range due to the bushwhacking required.

Trailhead access: On Route 430, approximately 28 kilometres past the visitor centre, park in the large parking area for Western Brook Pond: 49.7882564, -57.870836. Do the loop in either direction (hike in via Snug Harbour, boat out via Western Brook Pond, or vice versa).

Amenities: Outhouse and picnic tables at parking area; washrooms and concession at dock. Some backcountry campsites have wooden platforms, pit toilets, and food lockers or bear poles.

Keep in mind:

■ This is not a marked trail. Do not rely solely on GPS. Be sure you are proficient with map and compass and have a topographic map.

■ Visibility may be greatly reduced in fog and may force you to stop hiking to wait it out.

■ You will receive a transceiver from the park: return it at the end of your hike. Bring an emergency communication device: a marine radio, satellite phone, or SPOT. Cell phones do not work.

■ There are many stream crossings and Western Brook may be too high to cross early in the spring. Check with park staff for current conditions.

■ Cook and store food away from camp to discourage black bears.

■ Campfires are not permitted.

■ Don't be fooled: Herds of caribou and moose make paths all over the mountains. Stick to your map route.

Permits & fees

■ Book hiking dates in advance to avoid disappointment; there is a small window of good hiking weather.

■ Arrive at least one day before your departure to attend a mandatory pre-trip planning session, which includes a map and compass skills assessment.

■ Reservation and backcountry camping fees apply.

■ When booking hiking dates, book boat tickets as well (see information at the back of this book).

Map #: 12 H/12 and 12 H/13

Cow Head

Cow Head Lighthouse Trail leads to a small lighthouse that was built in 1909. In 1960, it became automated; it is no longer in use. From the lighthouse, you may continue along the trail onto the coast at Sandy Point. Walk among the 500-million-year-old breccias that make up the beach.

The next trail leads out to Cow Head. You can access the beach from the head when the tide is right. All trails are well-marked and -maintained. The trails wind through tuckamore, meadows, and coastline. There is no major elevation gain, only one small 60-metre hill.

The tip of the trail offers incredible views of the coastline and ocean, along with interesting rock formations. Look for whales and berries.

The coastline, formed of 500-million-year-old rocks, is a geologist's paradise.

You may notice archaeological dig sites along the trails. These 4,000-year-old sites are from three different groups: Maritime Archaic, Dorset Eskimo, and Groswater Paleoeskimo.

Distance: 4-kilometre loop.

Trailhead access: Exit Route 430 into Cow Head. From Main Street turn onto Pond Road, which takes you onto the peninsula (the head). Stay left and park by the community outdoor theatre near the communication tower: 49.9196649, -57.8141024.

Amenities: Outhouses in parking area; viewing platforms along the trails.

Keep in mind: Watch the tide if exploring the beaches or rocky outcrops—don't get stranded! The coastline's exposure to wind and waves can create a dangerous environment.

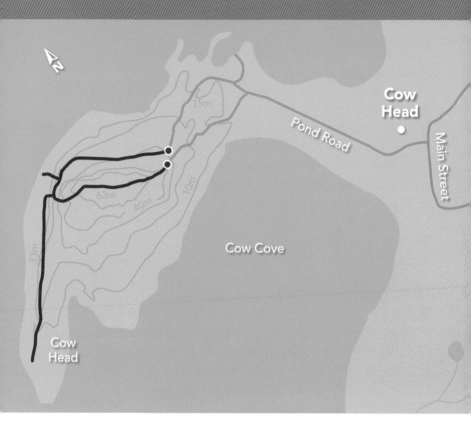

NORTHERN PENINSULA

Commonly referred to as "The Great Northern Peninsula," this region boasts some of the most rugged and dramatic landscapes on the island. The coastline is home to many of Newfoundland's wonders: towering cliffs, Viking ruins, and whale and iceberg sightings. In fact, where the tip of the Northern Peninsula reaches out into the Labrador Current is known worldwide as Iceberg Alley, spectacular for its annual parade of glassy blue ice giants. Hiking along the shore in late spring and even throughout the summer will bring you to small coves and bays where icebergs may be grounded or bergy bits scattered on the beaches.

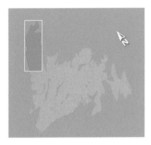

This region is also steeped in history. Visit L'Anse aux Meadows National Historic Site to see where the Vikings landed, Conche to admire the French Shore Tapestry, and St. Anthony to explore the Grenfell Historic Properties. Local residents love to share stories and are eager to tell you about how life was; many have lived through the closure of the cod fishery and their lives have undergone dramatic shifts in response to the subsequent economic collapse.

The Northern Peninsula is rugged and remote, with many unique features. Enjoy the beauty of the small communities, the landscape, the marine environment, and the warmth of the people you meet while you explore this region by foot.

Trails of the Northern Peninsula

35. Devil's Bite Trail / Parson's Pond
36. Indian Lookout Trail / Portland Creek
37. Point Riche Lighthouse Trail / Port au Choix
38. Englee Trail Network / Englee
39. French Shore Trail / Conche
40. Conche Trail Network / Conche
41. Treena's Trail / Ship Cove
42. Whale Point Trail / Wild Bight

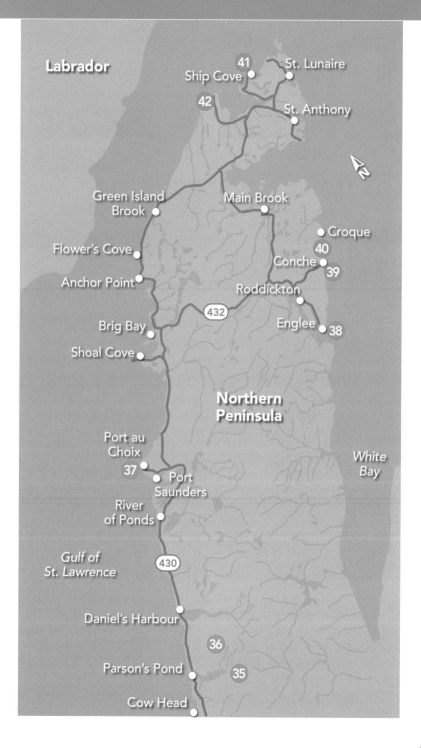

Labrador

41 Ship Cove

St. Lunaire

42

St. Anthony

Green Island Brook

Main Brook

Croque

40

Conche

39

Flower's Cove

Roddickton

Anchor Point

432

Brig Bay

Englee

38

Shoal Cove

Northern Peninsula

Port au Choix

37

White Bay

Port Saunders

River of Ponds

Gulf of St. Lawrence

430

Daniel's Harbour

36

Parson's Pond

35

Cow Head

Parson's Pond

*This is a backcountry route, **not** a maintained trail; most hikers take three to four days (two or three nights in a tent) to complete it. This description is based on hiking the loop counter-clockwise.*

Devil's Bite Trail brings adventurous hikers to the remote landlocked fjord of Inner Parson's Pond and passes some of the area's largest waterfalls. You must be shuttled by fishing boat to the trailhead—sit back and absorb the view during the ride.

From the trailhead, hike up and into Western Brook Gulch. As you ascend, you'll pass the 300-metre waterfall of Western Brook (of Parson's Pond) Gulch. When crossing from Western Brook Gulch to Parson's Pond Inner Pond Gulch, take an 8-kilometre round-trip side trek to the Devil's Bite landmark and

lookout. Head next into Parson's Pond Inner Pond Valley and to beautiful Freake's Falls. Cross the stream above the falls, then hike to the top of Parson's Pinnacle to view the surrounding mountains and valleys.

After Parson's Pinnacle, descend into and cross Corner Pond Valley. The trail then rises along the eastern rim of Parson's Pond Inner Pond Gulch, affording unsurpassed views from the sheer 600-metre cliffs of Inner and Outer Parson's Ponds, the Devil's Bite, and the distant Gulf of St. Lawrence. The trail then encircles Main Gulch and Little Gulch before winding around and down the northern corner of East Brook Gulch and back toward Parson's Pond and the north Middle Brook trailhead.

> Local residents refer to the jagged ridge visible throughout most of the hike as Devil's Bite, said to be created when the devil bit into the mountain precipice.

The Arches
Provincial
Park

430

Parson's
Pond

Outer
Parson's Pond

Inner
Parson's Pond

Distance: 45-kilometre loop.

Trailhead access: From the community of Parson's Pond, take a 14-kilometre boat shuttle to the trailhead. The trailheads are both at Middle Brook (one to the south, one to the north). Middle Brook connects Parson's Pond Inner and Outer Ponds (labelled Parson's Pond River on some maps). You'll need to arrange a return shuttle. Contact IATNL for shuttle arrangements and GPS references and route track.

Amenities: Cabins for rent at the trailhead; no facilities on the trails.

Keep in mind: This trek involves many creek crossings; bring a second pair of footwear and unbuckle your pack when crossing. The trail traverses steep cliffs; stay back from the edges. The only access to this remote high country is this trail or by skidoo in winter.

Map #: 12H13 & 12H14

Permits & fees: Donations toward trail upkeep, payable to IATNL, are encouraged.

Portland Creek

*This is a backcountry route, **not** a maintained trail; most hikers take three to four days (two or three nights in a tent) to complete it. This description is based on hiking the loop counter-clockwise.*

> The barren subarctic mountain plateau and surrounding area is home to Arctic hare, partridge, caribou, moose, rock ptarmigan, and, occasionally, black bear.

Distance: 40-kilometre loop.

Trailhead access: About 2.5 kilometres south of Arches Provincial Park on Route 430 (halfway between the communities of Parson's Pond and Portland Creek), turn onto Five Mile Road, a 9-kilometre gravel road. Only the first half of the road is passable by car; the rest is accessible only by SUV, pickup, ATV, or foot. Contact IATNL for GPS references and route track.

Amenities: None.

Keep in mind: For the many creek crossings, bring a second pair of footwear and unbuckle your pack when crossing. The trail traverses steep cliffs; stay back from the edges. Map and compass skills required.

Map #: 12I4 & 12I3

Permits & fees: Donations toward trail upkeep, payable to IATNL, are encouraged.

Beginning at the trailhead sign off Five Mile Road, follow the trail to the fork and stay right. From the fork, the trail rises 640 metres to the summit of Flat Hills. This vantage point offers a sweeping view of the Gulf of St. Lawrence coastline from Bonne Bay to the Highlands of St. John, overlooking Port au Choix.

Follow the eastern ridge above Southwest Feeder Gulch to Indian Lookout. Indian Lookout provides views of the inland fjord of Portland Creek Inner Pond as well as Portland Creek Outer Pond and the Gulf of St. Lawrence. From Southwest Feeder Gulch you'll see steep verdurous cliffs and towering waterfalls, including the 400-metre Partridge Pond Falls.

The return trek to Five Mile Road via the north side of Southwest Feeder Gulch provides more scenic views of lakes and waterfalls. Rejoin the trail back to Five Mile Road at the fork.

The Arches Provincial Park

Portland Creek Pond

Inner Pond

Indian Lookout

Portland Creek

430

Port au Choix

The Point Riche Lighthouse Trail network is made up of several interconnecting trails. Leaving the lighthouse parking area, the Coastal Trail follows the limestone coast, where hikers can look for fossils of ancient sea life found nowhere else in Canada. This trail passes Philip's Garden, a Paleoeskimo archaeological site. Along this section are statues depicting Aboriginal ways of life.

Maritime Archaic Indians, the Groswater and Dorset Paleoeskimo, and the Recent Indians (ancestors of the Beothuks) once lived in this area. These archeological sites are 5,000 years old.

From Philip's Garden, continue on the Coastal Trail toward Old Port au Choix and the Philip Drive trailhead or walk through the archeological site and connect with the Dorset Trail, which will take you inland through stunted spruce forest and past small ponds and back to the visitor information centre.

The trails are well-maintained with gentle elevation changes. A few caribou live on this peninsula; if you are lucky enough to see these majestic animals, please keep a safe distance from them.

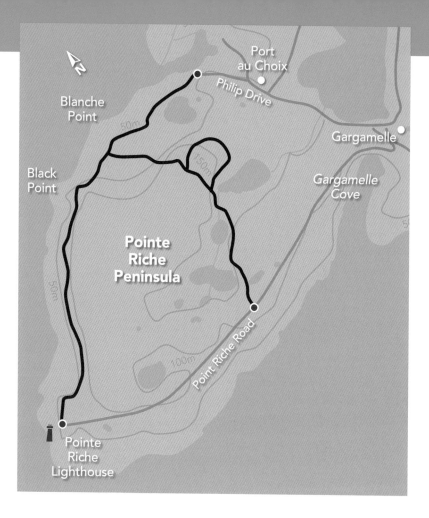

Distance:
10-kilometre trail network.

Trailhead access: Parking and trailheads are at the visitor information centre, the Point Riche Lighthouse (50.6989439, -57.40905), and in Old Port au Choix on Philip Drive (50.7168682, -57.369876).

Amenities: Visitor information centre, outhouses, picnic tables, and interpretation panels.

Keep in mind: This trail is along exposed coastline; winds and waves can be extreme. Fossils are not to be removed or collected from this or any site.

Permits & fees: Pay a day fee to enter this National Historic Site or purchase a Viking Trail pass, which provides entry to Gros Morne National Park, L'Anse aux Meadows, Red Bay, Port au Choix National Historic Site, and the Grenfell Historic Properties provincial site, valid for seven consecutive days.

Englee

The Englee Trail Network has four trails, totalling 4.7 kilometres, which can be hiked separately or, if you connect them by walking through the community, all together.

■ White Point Trail is a linear, 1.5-kilometre (3-kilometre return) trail with lookout points spanning the west side of Englee Island.

■ A 0.7-kilometre loop encircling Barr'd Island, Barr'd Island Trail has many stairs and views of Englee Harbour and Canada Bay. In season, you may even see icebergs or whales.

■ Locker's Point Trail is a 1.5-kilometre (3-kilometre return) linear traverse of the mountains behind the community. This trail has strenuous uphill sections. Three lookouts are on the trail, including the 120-metre George's Lookout, accessed by a side trail. At Locker's Point, check out the ridges and beds of sandstone, marble, schist, and limestone.

■ The 1-kilometre (2-kilometre return) linear Shoe Pond Trail starts as an easy walk but quickly rises before you reach the gazebo at the top of Eastern Hill and views of Englee, Canada Bay, and Bide Arm.

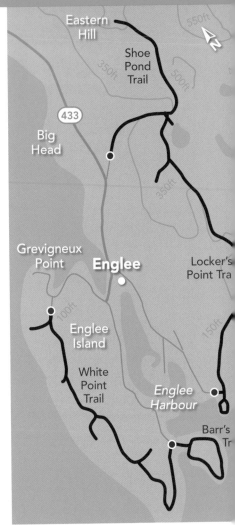

Distance:
See trail description above.

Trailhead access:

White Point Trail: This trail has two access points:

■ From Main Street, turn right and cross the bridge, then turn right onto Heights Cove Road and drive past the fish plant. Take the next left and park at the top of the road: 50.731190, -56.112956.

■ Barr'd Island Trail trailhead.

Barr'd Island Trail:

■ From Main Street, turn right, cross the bridge, then turn left onto Marine Side Drive and drive to the end. Park at the trail signs: 50.723323, -56.109747.

Locker's Point: This trail has two access points:

■ From Main Street turn left at the stop sign onto Dorset Drive. Follow to the end: 50.737560, -56.096992. Park at the trail sign, then walk along the gravel road past the last house and around the point. The trail heads into the forest and into the hills.

■ Shoe Pond trailhead.

Shoe Pond Trail:

■ Turn off Main Street onto Macdonald Drive. If you are driving a small car, park by the basketball court. Otherwise, drive straight but stay left at any intersections until you see the trailhead sign: 50.737789, -56.096321.

Amenities: Gazebos or platforms at lookouts.

Keep in mind: Be mindful of high winds, cliff edges, and tides.

Conche

*This is a backcountry route, **not** a maintained trail; most hikers take two days (one night in a tent) to complete it. This description is based on hiking in from Southwest Crouse.*

The French Shore Trail is a 13-kilometre linear trail along the eastern coastline of the Northern Peninsula between Conche and Croque, two communities on the historic French Shore. Watch for cairns, of unknown origin, which dot the trail.

The trail begins at the communication tower off Route 434 overlooking the communities of Conche and Southwest Crouse, follows the rolling seaside hills north, and takes hikers out onto the Cape Rouge Peninsula. Along the way are views of the surrounding headlands, coves, islands, and ocean, as well as the abandoned fishing communities which dot Crouse Harbour.

From a sheltered campsite on the northern shore of Crouse Harbour, the trail climbs about 170 metres to a scenic lookout at Pyramid Point on the northern end of Cape Rouge Peninsula. The trail then winds across barren hilltops north until it reaches a stream-fed cove halfway between Conche and Croque. Hikers can choose to return via the same route or arrange a boat shuttle to return to Southwest Crouse.

In the early 1500s French fishermen crossed the Atlantic in pursuit of the large cod stocks around Newfoundland, particularly in the waters off its northern coast—thus the area became known as the French Shore.

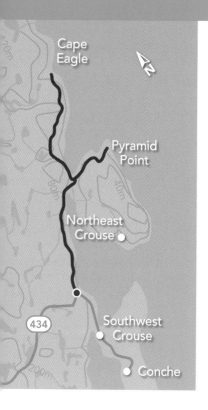

Distance: 13-kilometre linear trail (26-kilometre return).

Trailhead access: Take Route 434 toward Conche. Before the main road descends into Southwest Crouse, turn onto a short gravel road leading to a communication tower. Boat transportation can be arranged through IATNL for drop-off or pickup at the northern end. Contact IATNL for GPS references and route tracks.

Amenities: None.

Keep in mind: This is a very remote area. The best communication option is marine radio, as local mariners or the coast guard would be the first on the scene in an emergency. Map and compass skills required.

Map #: 2L13

Permits & fees: Donations toward trail upkeep, payable to IATNL, are encouraged.

Conche

The landscape around Conche and Crouse is criss-crossed with rough hiking trails and some boardwalks, which can be hiked together or in segments depending on your available time and fitness level.

■ Sleepy Cove Trail, a 2.5-kilometre linear trail, traverses Martinique Bay and affords hikers picturesque views of the village of Conche and its harbour.

■ The fully boardwalked Captain Coublongue Trail, an easily accessed 3-kilometre linear trail, takes hikers to Point Dos de Cheval and a lookout offering panoramic views of Southwest Crouse Harbour and the Cape Rouge Peninsula.

■ Fox Head Trail offers spectacular views along high cliffs with broad views of neighbouring islands and landforms. Along the 7-kilometre trail, be sure to check out Glass Hole, Cape Fox Archaeology Site, Saunders Gulch Lookout, and Conche Lookout. To return, retrace your steps on Fox Head Trail or complete a loop, passing through a World War II plane-crash site. You may also continue all the way to the Captain Coublongue Trailhead.

Return via the main road through the community or pre-arrange a shuttle.

Distance:
12.5-kilometre trail network.

Trailhead access:

■ In Southwest Crouse, off Route 434, park by Captain Coublongue's gravesite: 50.9015988, -55.8906291.

■ Walk back along the road into Southwest Crouse until you see Sleepy Cove Trail: 50.9044603, -55.8924412.

■ In Conche, turn left before the town wharf and park at the end of the road to access Fox Head Trail. The other trailhead begins near the World War II plane-crash site: 50.8834253, -55.8965324.

Amenities: None.

Keep in mind: Trails along the eastern side of the peninsula are on steep cliffs; stay on marked trails. It may be very windy or rainy along this shore at any time of the year; dress accordingly.

Map #: 2L13

Permits & fees: Donations to trail upkeep are payable to the French Shore Historical Society.

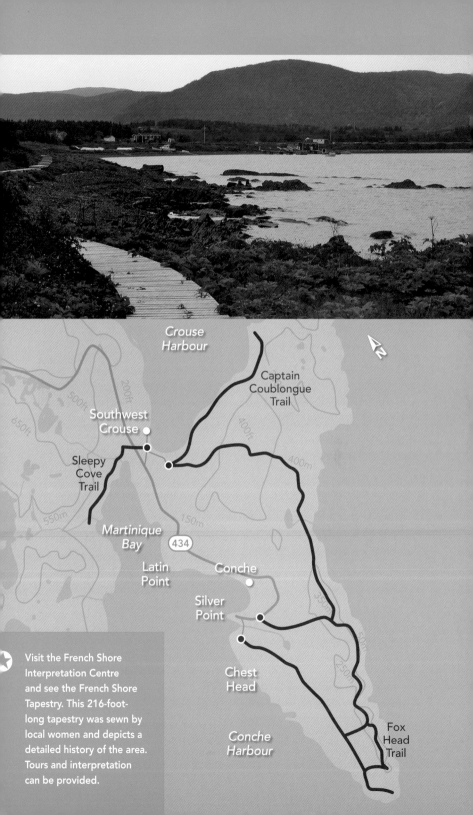

Crouse
Harbour

Captain
Coublongue
Trail

Southwest
Crouse

Sleepy
Cove
Trail

Martinique
Bay

434

Latin
Point

Conche

Silver
Point

Chest
Head

Conche
Harbour

Fox
Head
Trail

Visit the French Shore
Interpretation Centre
and see the French Shore
Tapestry. This 216-foot-
long tapestry was sewn by
local women and depicts a
detailed history of the area.
Tours and interpretation
can be provided.

Ship Cove

From the parking area, cross Route 437 to the blue sign that says "Back of the Land Trail." Treena's Trail begins here. Follow the quad track to Savage Cove, then head right as the trail climbs the 80-metre-high hills. You will see orange wooden trail markers and blue signs indicating the lookouts.

The quad trail eventually veers, and hikers should stay on the footpath heading toward Cape Onion. At Cape Onion, the trail passes by two houses—stay left of them and head toward the cemetery. A short side trail leads to a lookout; the main trail continues through the cemetery parking area and follows the road down toward the water. Walk along the road, following the shoreline, until you see the "mini village"—replicas of the first church in Ship Cove, a general store, a lighthouse, and more.

★ An exhibit depicting Ship Cove's heritage, by photographer Paul-Émile Miot (1827-1900), is displayed in the community. Miot was an officer in the French Navy; his photographs were the earliest photographic records of Atlantic Canada.

Continue past an old house and up into a driveway. Walk out the driveway, turn left, and continue to a blue bus-shelter-type structure. Turn right on the quad trail and follow it along the shore until it turns right onto Route 437. The parking lot will be within view.

Distance: 7-kilometre loop.

Trailhead access: Take Route 437 toward Ship Cove. About 1 kilometre before Ship Cove, park in the designated area beside a blue trailhead sign: 51.6012365, -55.6514616. The trail may also be accessed from the end of the road in Cape Onion or from the Ship Cove Cemetery.

Amenities: Lookouts, mini village.

Keep in mind: Stay back from cliff edges. Moose and coyote live in the area; dogs should be leashed.

Onion
Cove

Diable
Cove

Ship
Cove

Low
Islands

Little
Harbour

437

Savage
Cove

Point Road

Fauvette
Point

250ft

150ft

150ft

100ft

100ft

150ft

100ft

150ft

Wild Bight

Whale Point Trail leads along limestone barrens, past Soup Bay, and out to Whale Point. The trail has little elevation change and is easy to follow— no trees obstruct the view.

At Whale Point, take some time to watch the water and you might be graced with a visit by a whale. Take the stairs from the point and follow the trail through the gravel pit and over to Cape Norman to the lighthouse and viewing gazebo.

The Cape Norman area is designated a "critical habitat" because of the rare species barrens willow and Fernald's braya, which are only found in this region. As you walk along the trail, look for these plants. Return to the trailhead via the Whale Point trail or walk back on the lighthouse access road.

> ★ Whale Point was so named for the many whale-watching opportunities it offers, particularly during summer migration, when whales frequently feed in the area.

Distance: 4-kilometre linear trail (8-kilometre return).

Trailhead access: Take Route 435 through Wild Bight; after the last house, park by the trailhead sign on the right: 51.6116357, -55.9025071.

Amenities: Benches, picnic tables, information signs, gazebos.

Keep in mind: Where this trail allows access to the water, consider changes in the tides. Remember: the limestone barrens of this area are protected by federal laws. Stay on designated trails.

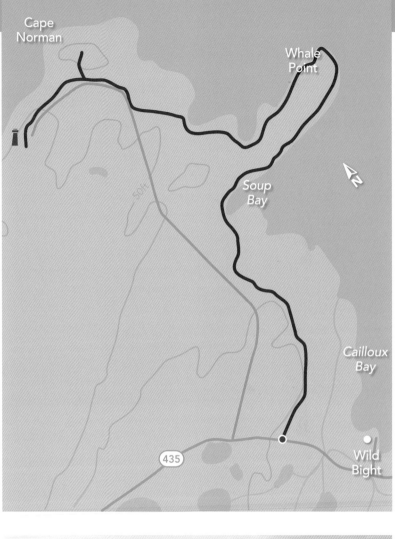

Cape
Norman

Whale
Point

Soup
Bay

Cailloux
Bay

Wild
Bight

435

N

CENTRAL NEWFOUNDLAND: BAIE VERTE & TWILLINGATE

This is your guide to those trails of central Newfoundland from Deer Lake eastward, including the Baie Verte Peninsula and the many islands along the northeastern shore up to Twillingate. *Hikes of Eastern Newfoundland* profiles trails east of Twillingate, including Fogo Island and Change Islands.

Central Newfoundland boasts at least 55 marked trails, 19 of which are listed below and described in this book, that take hikers along rocky coasts, into secluded beaches, and through communities where wharves, boats, and fishing gear testify to the centuries-old fishing industry and its continued importance in the twenty-first century. The region is visited annually by 26 species of whales and six types of icebergs.

The region has a rich Aboriginal history that dates to 5,000 years ago and includes the Dorset people and, later, the Beothuks. Most residents of the central north shore are descendants of West Country (England) fishers who worked along this coast, beginning in the sixteenth century. Botwood and Gander also played an important role during World War II as landing destinations for transatlantic flights.

Trails of Central Newfoundland: Baie Verte & Twillingate

43. Hummock Trail / Fleur de Lys
44. Ocean View Trail / Pacquet
45. Alexander Murray Trail / King's Point
46. Ocean View Trail / Jackson's Cove
47. Trail with a View / Harry's Harbour
48. Indian River Walking Trail / Springdale
49. Hazelnut Hiking & Adventure Trail / Robert's Arm
50. Beothuk Hiking Trail / Beaumont North (Long Island)
51. Maple Ridge Hiking Trail / Triton

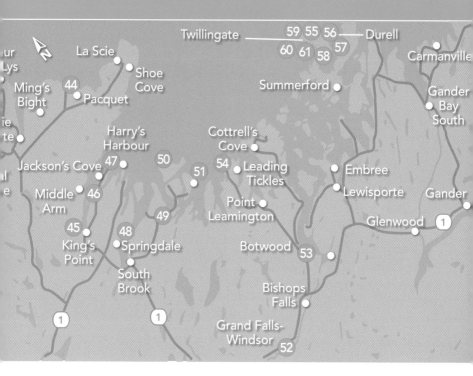

2 Fleur de Lys

The Hummock Trail, well-marked by red arrows and signs, has an easy start, winding pleasantly through the forest. Some sections cross bogs, which are quite muddy and soft: stay on the boardwalks.

The next section is the toughest part of the trail. You'll gain elevation quickly—but it's worth the climb. At the top are two lookouts, each about 200 metres high, overlooking the community of Fleur de Lys and parts of White Bay. Icebergs are plentiful early in the summer. Enjoy the descent, made easier by stairs.

This trail exhibits rich boreal forest flora and fauna. The ground is covered with a variety of small boreal plants and pleasant-smelling flowers. Pitcher plants are also seen. Be wary of the high population of moose, especially on the trail's lower section; you are likely to encounter one or spot its tracks. The trail ends as it intersects with Route 410. Turn right and walk about 500 metres to the cemetery and parking area.

★ Dorset Paleoeskimos lived in this area. Visit the Dorset Soapstone Quarry Interpretation Centre to find out more about their way of life.

Distance: 4-kilometre loop.

Trailhead access: On Route 410, before Fleur de Lys, watch for a large trail sign and parking area beside a cemetery on the left: 50.1183997, -56.1569853. The start of the trail is located at the end of the old baseball field on a quad trail.

Amenities: Picnic tables and lookout platforms along the trail; swimming area across from the cemetery.

Keep in mind: Fallen trees on the trail may require short detours. The ascent has a steep section without stairs; this may be slippery and challenging in the spring and after heavy rain.

Permits & fees: Donations toward trail upkeep are payable to the Town of Fleur de Lys.

1 Pacquet

To complete a full loop of the Ocean View Trail network, start on the path without a sign (i.e., not Chelsey's Lookout). This trail starts in the forest with a gentle descent to a rocky beach before reaching the coast and views of Iceberg Alley.

Eventually the trail leads to Chelsey's Lookout, overlooking the surrounding cliffs and ocean. Continue up to Uncle Billy's Lookout, where a colony of gulls nest. You'll likely hear or smell the seabirds before you see them. With binoculars, you may glimpse the chicks, as they hang on to the cliff edges.

Most of the trail is fairly flat, except for a short climb to reach

These trails provide opportunities for viewing whales, icebergs, and a rich variety of seabirds. Some rocks in the area portray the wavy sedimentary layers formed by tectonic activity.

Uncle Billy's Lookout. Multiple trails make it easy to tailor a hike to the hiker's strength and available time. Use the interpretation panel of the trails, located at the intersection of the dirt road, to plan a route.

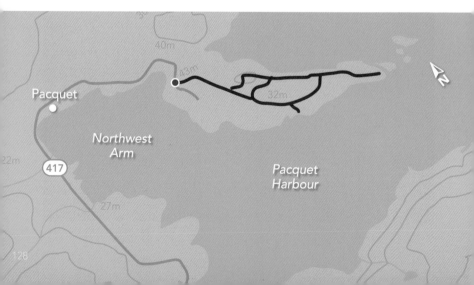

Distance:
8-kilometre trail network.

Trailhead access: Take Route 417 through Pacquet until you see a wooden sign with a fleur de lys on it. Turn left and follow the signs on the dirt road to a parking area: 49.9886775, -55.8660799.

Amenities: Outhouses, picnic tables, lookout platforms, and a gazebo.

Keep in mind: Most of the coast is exposed to White Bay and the area can be windy. During storms or when the surf is high, stay away from the cliffs; waves are unpredictable and can be dangerous.

King's Point

The first 2 kilometres of the Alexander Murray Trail meander through the forest with short stairs and boardwalks. The trail then opens up into barrens with short, stunted trees and a view of the lookout and stairs ahead. Watch for moose in the barrens on this first section of the trail.

When the trail splits, go left or right (this part of the trail is a loop) to reach the Hay Pook Lookout, the summit of the trail, at 335 metres. This challenging section climbs steeply, but a total of 2,200 stairs will help you get to the top. If you go left at the fork, the first stairs are located under the forest canopy, which offers some shade.

Take the short side trail to the bottom of the 182-metre Corner Brook Falls and gorge, particularly spectacular after a spring snow melt or

> ★ These trails provide opportunities for viewing whales, icebergs, and a rich variety of seabirds. Some rocks in the area portray the wavy sedimentary layers formed by tectonic activity.

heavy rains. The waterfall and pool are perfect for a swim in the heat of summer. This is a linear trail offshoot and you'll need to hike back up the stairs to continue the loop.

From the top, enjoy the landscapes of Green Bay, Gaff Topsails, and Mount Sykes. The summit also overlooks barrens and perhaps a caribou herd. Early in the summer season (May–June), icebergs float down into the bay. Return through the forest, where another waterfall awaits you. Finish the loop and return to the parking area via the linear section.

Distance: 8-kilometre loop.

Trailhead access: Take Route 391 toward King's Point. Just before the community, turn left at the sign, near several red buildings: 49.5847, -56.1805.

Amenities: Washrooms and maps at the interpretation centre; viewing platforms and picnic tables along the trail.

Keep in mind: Some stairs and boardwalks need maintenance and are unstable; the stairs are slippery when wet.

Permits & fees: Donations accepted toward trail upkeep via a donation box at the trail entrance.

1 Jackson's Cove

Ocean View Trail takes hikers through a short section of forest before following the gentle coastline; it includes boardwalk sections and stairs. Three major lookout platforms along the trail provide views of Green Bay and the Baie Verte Peninsula across the bay. Whales, icebergs, and seabirds are frequently sighted.

Can you spot the sea arch? Wait until the end of the trail to look— you won't miss it, unless the day is foggy with poor visibility. From the last viewing platform, you can head down to the ocean, but be extremely wary in stormy weather and crashing waves. On a bright, sunny, calm day, you may find the salt water refreshing.

Return to the parking area by the same route.

> ★ The coastline by Ocean View Trail is rich in flora and fauna and, in season, icebergs.

Distance: 2.5-kilometre linear trail (5-kilometre return).

Trailhead access: Follow Route 391 northward. Turn left toward Jackson's Cove and turn right at the next intersection. The trailhead and small parking area are on the left, just after the Jackson's Cove sign: 49.6913407, -55.9849749.

Amenities: Lookout platforms and picnic tables.

Keep in mind: This area, exposed to the ocean, may be very windy.

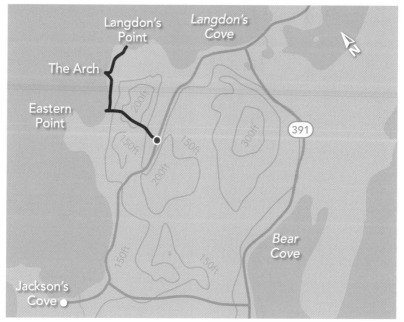

Harry's Harbour

Pack a picnic and spend an afternoon—even a full day—walking this trail network and swimming in the coves. The trails have little elevation gain but can become a moderate hike if you explore all 9 kilometres. The main trail is inland, with multiple shorter trails branching off toward the coast. Each short trail leads to a cove, beach, or lookout. The main trail is shared with quads, but some of the trails heading to coves are much narrower and only accessible to hikers.

From the lookout, whales are often spotted as well as an osprey pair that has a nest on top of a rock pillar. Unobstructed views of the shoreline and fascinating rock formations await at each cove. Parts of the trails are boardwalk; a few sections may be interrupted by fallen trees that you'll have to walk around.

Forest, valleys, and beach landscapes offer a diversity of scenery and make this trail a good option for hikers of all ages and interests.

Seabirds and whales are spotted from this trail. Sea stars and sea urchins are also plentiful in many of the coves by the rocky shoreline.

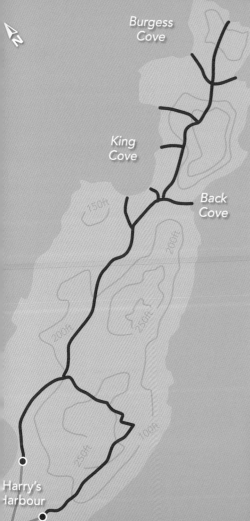

Burgess Cove

King Cove

Back Cove

150ft
200ft
250ft
200ft
250ft
200ft
100ft
250ft
100ft

Harry's Harbour

Distance:
9-kilometre trail network.

Trailhead access: Take Route 391 to Harry's Harbour. Drive to the end of the main road and turn left across from the church onto the street to Salmon Cove: 49.702841, -55.9228888.

Park by the trail sign; the trailhead is on the right.

Amenities: Outhouses, picnic tables, and lookout platforms along the trail; a shelter at the trailhead.

Keep in mind: The trail that heads to the lookout has many fallen trees. Faded or washed-out signs may be difficult to read.

Springdale

The wetlands and river along the Indian River Walking Trail are the natural habitat of many animals, including birds which come to nest and feed. Be sure to bring binoculars.

From the Main Street trailhead, the trail is fairly flat as it follows a marsh, then the Indian River, and meanders through the forest. The last section,

toward George Huxter Memorial Park, has more elevation change, made easy with a few short sets of stairs.

The trail, which traverses a landscape of waterfalls flowing over mafic volcanic rocks, was once farther inland; it has been remade, so stay on the new route, closest to the water. New housing and roads force the hiker onto the road at a few locations. When this happens, keep walking down the road in the direction you were heading and you'll find another entrance with garbage bins and/or signs.

Return the way you came, arrange a shuttle, or leave a vehicle at each end.

> ★ The sand at the mouth of the Indian River and around Springdale was pushed and left there 18,000 years ago during the last ice age.
>
> The Indian River flows into Notre Dame Bay and salmon migrate upstream every year. Be sure to visit the salmon ladder by the park.

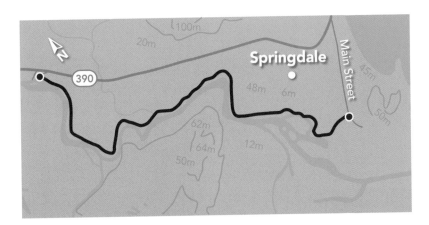

Distance: 6-kilometre linear trail (12-kilometre return).

Trailhead access: Take Route 390 to Springdale.

■ The first trailhead is located off Route 390 at George Huxter Memorial Park: 49.5113551, -56.1091237.

■ For the Main Street trailhead, drive through Springdale, turn right onto Main Street, drive almost to the end of the street, and park beside the trail sign: 49.4900631, -56.0744184.

Amenities: Washrooms and campsites at the park; benches, gazebos, lookouts, picnic tables, and storyboards and interpretation signs along the trail.

Keep in mind: Some sections of trail are not well-marked.

Permits & fees: Donations toward trail upkeep are payable to the Town of Springdale.

Robert's Arm

This trail has a feature unlike any other in this province: a chance to see Cressie, the monster of Crescent Lake, similar to the Loch Ness Monster. Aboriginal legends tell stories about a "pond devil" or "swimming monster." In 2008, the History Channel's "Monster Quest" aired an episode about Cressie; sightings have placed the eel-like creature between 2 and 5 metres long. Crescent Lake is 100 metres deep and connects to Robert's Arm Harbour on the southeast side, which would allow such a creature to enter the lake and offer it plenty of depth in which to hide.

Most of the Hazelnut Trail is flat and follows the shores of Crescent Lake. An optional climb of 130 metres to Hazelnut Hill offers a view of Robert's Arm, Crescent Lake, and Long Pond. Sections of the trail follow beaches, perfect for a summer swim (for those not afraid of Cressie); other sections

Distance:
10-kilometre trail network.

Trailhead access: Take Route 380 toward Robert's Arm. The trailhead is on the right-hand side by Crescent Lake, just before the town: 49.4888783, -55.8312226.

Amenities: Gazebos, picnic tables, benches, outhouses, interpretation panels, and lookout platforms along the trail.

Keep in mind: Watch for Cressie the lake monster.

Permits & fees: Donations toward trail upkeep are payable to the Town of Robert's Arm.

lead through the forest. The trail is well-maintained, with boardwalks and bridges.

The trail circumnavigates the lake and ends at a dirt road. Stay left until you reach the main road (Route 380), and head left, toward the parking lot. Make this trail shorter by heading straight up Hazelnut Hill and returning to the parking lot, or longer by completing the entire trail and walking back along the road.

Sign the visitors' book on your way out and share your stories, sightings, or feedback.

Logging was the main industry in this area in the early 1930s. Pulp and paper mills were abundant and, until the 1980s, Newfoundland supplied Bowater-Lloyd (Europe's largest newsprint manufacturer) in London, England, with most of its raw material.

1 Beaumont North (Long Island)

A stroll along a boardwalk through forests and bogs brings you to a set of stairs, and then up and out to Western Head. These bogs are home to the carnivorous pitcher plant, which turns bright red by the end of summer. Look for the beaver dam along the trail.

From the gazebo at Western Head, take in the panoramic view of Beaumont North and surrounding islands. In season, this is an ideal location for whale and iceberg sightings.

Follow the shoreline toward Caplin Cove Head. The stairs up to Caplin Cove Head are the last of the hike, and the 360-degree view of Long Island is worth the climb. The vast

> This coastal area was an ideal summer destination for Beothuks to fish and hunt—until the Europeans arrived and eventually pushed the Beothuks inland, contributing to their eventual extinction. Read the interpretation panels along the trail to learn more about the Beothuks and the artifacts that were found here.

horizon gives opportunities for photos, particularly at sunrise and sunset. From Caplin Cove Head you can see China Head, where hundreds of Beothuk Indian artifacts were found.

Return to the parking lot along the same trail.

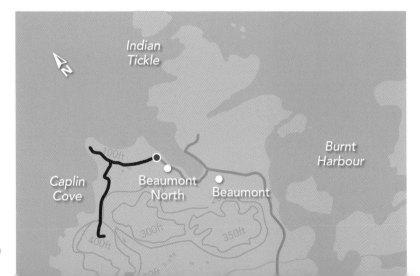

Distance: 2.5-kilometre linear trail (5-kilometre return).

Trailhead access: Follow Route 380 toward the Long Island ferry (turn left in the community of Pilley's Island). After a five-minute ferry crossing, drive to the end of the road at Beaumont North Harbour, and turn left along the bay, following the trail signs. Park at the end of the road: 49.6230138, -55.6895646.

Amenities: Gazebos and picnic tables along the trail.

Keep in mind: This trail is exposed to the ocean—beware of high winds and cliff edges.

Triton

Get ready for stairs! Most of this trail is stairs—all the way up and all the way back down. But first, the trail passes a rocky beach where summer heat may tempt hikers for a swim.

After the beach comes a quick elevation gain through a forest of deciduous trees, with many maple trees, which are scarce on the island. At the lookout, a panoramic view of islands, mountains, Triton Harbour, and Notre Dame Bay awaits. Icebergs coming from Greenland and the Arctic may be seen from this vantage point during the spring and early summer. The 130-metre summit is perfect for a picnic and a well-deserved rest.

Walk back to the parking lot via the same trail. Most of the trail has either boardwalk or stairs; only a few sections are gravel-filled.

> ★ Coloured barrels in the bay belong to a mussel farm, a form of aquaculture that uses barrels from which ropes or "socks" of mussels are suspended vertically.

Distance: 2.5-kilometre linear trail (5-kilometre return).

Trailhead access: Follow Route 380 past Triton and turn left at the sign for Brighton. Shortly after the turn is a large trail sign on the right, beside a swimming pool. The trail starts by the gazebo: 49.5207422, -55.6268156.

Amenities: Gazebo, benches, and picnic tables along the trail.

Keep in mind: Stay hydrated and make several stops along the stairs.

Permits & fees: Donations toward trail upkeep are payable to the Town of Triton.

Grand Falls-Windsor

The walking trails in this network are flat, wide, and gravelled. If you want a challenge, follow the hiking trails, which are rougher and narrower.

In general, the trails follow Corduroy Brook and its watershed, taking hikers through the surrounding wetlands. Be sure to hike out to Corduroy Pond and Little Corduroy Pond, where an array of wildlife, including shorebirds, waterfowl, fish, and beavers, live.

Other trail highlights include Gibson's Field, the Wetlands, and the Lion's Playground. These trails are worthwhile for their interpretation panels, which turn the walk or hike into an outdoor educational

During the summer, many children's nature camps are held in and around the trails. Nature enthusiasts and bird watchers of all levels and ages will be rewarded with the rich and diversified fauna and flora of the wetlands.

experience. The panels highlight information about local animals, plants, tree rings, beaver lodges, and more.

Pick up a trail map for easier navigation, although you will find many maps along the trails. As it is in the centre of Grand Falls-Windsor, this rich and diversified trail system can lead to any length of trail you want to walk.

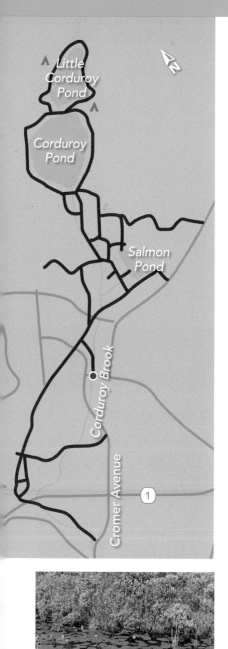

Distance: 16-kilometre trail network.

Trailhead access: Some trail access points are scattered around Grand Falls-Windsor. Stop at the interpretation centre just off Route 1 Exit 17 and pick up a town map to plan your hike. A good place to start is at the conservation centre: take Exit 18 and follow Cromer Avenue onto Earle Street, turn right on Queensway, and then right on Conservation Place: 48.9565712, -55.6458806.

Amenities: Benches, picnic tables, and interpretation panels on all trails; some tent sites, outhouses, and picnic shelters available.

Keep in mind: Be courteous to trail users. Dogs must be leashed; clean up after your pet.

Permits & fees: Donations toward trail upkeep are payable to the Corduroy Brook Enhancement Association.

Botwood

Seaside Walking Trail follows the Bay of Exploits along the water's edge. Located in the heart of Botwood, the trail parallels Water Street, offering a clear view of the Bay of Exploits and Botwood. This is a perfect walking trail for a mellow stroll, as it has no elevation change and is gravelled. It is a linear trail and you walk back to the parking lot by the same route.

The Killick Island Walking Trail is located by the marina and the Botwood Flying Museum. It follows a narrow piece of land before going around a small hill which overlooks the Bay of Exploits.

The Killick Island Walking Trail has a full-sized flying boat on display by the marina, the location of the first transatlantic flights. Visit the Botwood Flying Boat Museum and Heritage Museum, which highlight stories about the town.

Another short walking trail with a gazebo overlooking the town of Botwood and Bay of Exploits is located at the end of King's Road.

Distance: Seaside Walking Trail, 1.5-kilometre linear trail (3-kilometre return); Killick Island Walking Trail, 1-kilometre loop.

Trailhead access: For both trails, exit Route 1 at Botwood and follow Route 350, turning right on Water Street.

■ Seaside Walking Trail: Follow Water Street to Parsleys Road. Park by the water, where the seaside walk starts: 49.1286868, -55.3600319. You may also park at the other end of this trail on Circular Road or Staff Road.

■ Killick Island Walking Trail: Follow Water Street into Botwood and straight onto Church Road; park at the Botwood Heritage Park and Museum on your left: 49.1521262, -55.3418529.

Amenities: Benches along the water and a gazebo on top of Blueberry Hill (at the end of King's Road).

Keep in mind: These are walking, not hiking, trails.

Leading Tickles

Oceanside Nature Trail is well-marked with flagging tape. Starting from the main trailhead, the first section of the trail has boardwalks and stairs. This trail only has slight elevation changes as it wanders through the forest. Two lookouts, located close to the tip of the peninsula, offer views of Burnt Island, Thomas Rowsell Island, Seal Bay, and Notre Dame Bay.

As the trail approaches the Park Road trailhead, it veers inland, offering fewer viewpoints. Two beautiful rocky beaches, named Sprune Beach and Hannam's Cove Beach, are perfect for hikers looking to take a summertime swim.

This small town is still quite active in the fishing industry. In season, it is also an excellent place to watch for whales and icebergs.

Several species of seabirds, seals, and whales can be seen from the trail. Walk back the same way you came, or veer off from the trail and follow the road back to the parking area.

Distance:
3-kilometre trail network.

Trailhead access: Follow Route 350 through Leading Tickles South and over the bridge into Leading Tickles. The main trailhead is at the end of Route 350, where there is a parking area and a trail map: 49.501303, -55.4697246.

Amenities: Two lookouts and a few picnic tables along the trail.

Permits & fees: Donations toward trail upkeep are payable to the Town of Leading Tickles.

Burnt
Island

*Butler
Cove*

Leading
Tickles

Leading
Tickles
South

Cull
Island

350

Durrell (South Twillingate Island)

The French Beach to Spiller's Cove Trail network is well-marked with signs and maps. The trails primarily traverse barrens, but they also wander into the forest and over bogs. Slight elevation changes offer views of Twillingate Island and the dramatic landscapes of coastal cliffs.

These trails bring you close to a vast array of Arctic plants, tuckamore, and boreal plants. In May and June whales and icebergs are spotted around Twillingate Island.

Walk down to French Beach and/or Spiller's Cove Beach, both perfect for picnicking. Many rock formations, with nicknames such as Cobra Rock, are found along the coastline. On a clear day you can distinguish Long Point Lighthouse in the distance. Look for the osprey's nest on top of a rock pillar in Spiller's Cove.

There are several trail options, depending on your time and agenda. All are worthwhile; a well-planned hike may prevent you from doubling back on a trail you just completed.

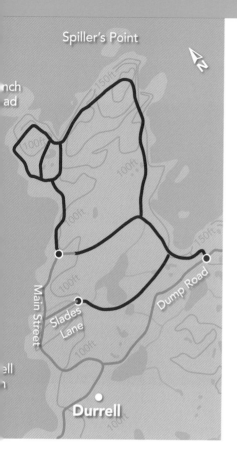

Spiller's Point

French Head

Main Street

Slades Lane

Dump Road

Durrell

Distance:
6.5-kilometre trail network.

Trailhead access:

◼ French Beach: Follow Route 340 to Twillingate and turn right on Main Street (toward Durrell), and drive to the end: 49.6684088, -54.7285534. Park by the trail map or nearby picnic tables.

◼ Spiller's Cove: From Main Street turn right onto Slades Lane or Dump Road and drive to the end: 49.6652783, -54.7295117.

Amenities: Benches and picnic tables along the trail.

Keep in mind: Avoid walking too close to cliff edges; cliffs may be undercut and unstable. High winds and wet conditions may be fatal in this terrain. Due to loose rock, hike carefully. Be wary of tides if accessing any of the beaches.

Permits & fees: Donations toward trail upkeep are payable to the Town of Twillingate.

2

Durrell (South Twillingate Island)

Spiller's Cove to Cod Jack's Cove Trail is a network of paths offering a few route options. In most cases, the paths are well-marked with signs and maps.

The trail access from Horwood Lane, however, can be confusing. From the trail map sign, follow the main logging road (there is a large pond on the right) and head straight to Cod Jack's Cove. From Cod Jack's Cove, the trail wanders through the forest and bogs to the tip of Clam Rock Head. Some sections are overgrown; when in doubt, follow the coast.

From Clam Rock Head, the trail traverses barrens toward Spiller's Cove and meanders along the rugged cliff edges. A few elevation changes bring you up to lookouts and down to beaches, including Spiller's Cove Beach.

Return by the same route or, to complete a loop, finish at French Beach and walk along Main Street back to Horwood Lane.

★ Watch for seabirds and osprey (there is an osprey nest on top of a rock pillar in Spiller's Cove), whales, and icebergs. The Arctic tundra-type terrain (the barrens) and boreal forests showcase a wide array of plant life.

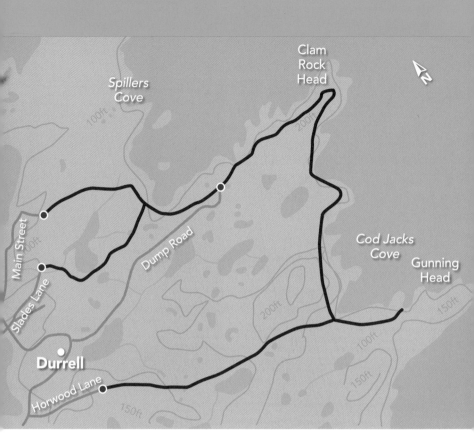

Distance:
6.5-kilometre trail network.

Trailhead access: Take Route 340 to Twillingate and turn right onto Main Street.

■ For Spiller's Cove trailhead, turn right onto Slades Lane or Dump Road and drive to the end: 49.6652783, -54.7295117.

■ To start at Cod Jack's Cove, turn right on Horwood Lane and park by the trail map: 49.658063, -54.7313802.

Amenities: Benches and picnic tables along the trail.

Keep in mind: Avoid getting too close to the edges of the steep, high cliffs along the trail. High winds and wet conditions make this landscape dangerous. Some sections of the trail have loose rock.

Permits & fees: Donations toward trail upkeep are payable to the Town of Twillingate.

2 Lower Little Harbour (South Twillingate Island)

Lower Little Harbour Trail, another trail network, includes both inland and coastal trails, each with stunning views.

If you're looking for a gentle walk or hike, try one (or both) of the two easiest sections of the trail network—one leading to the natural arch, the other heading toward Jonas Cove. Both travel over generally flat terrain; the trail to the arch follows a dirt road and also passes by a root cellar. If you hike down to the beach by the natural arch, be aware of changing tides and crashing waves.

The section of trail between the arch and Jonas Cove offers even greater views and elevation changes, which bring you to the top of the cliffs. Following the jagged coastline, the trail rewards hikers with views of Notre Dame Bay and Little Harbour before cutting back into the forest. In late summer, bakeapples may be found on this section of the trail. Return the same way you came in.

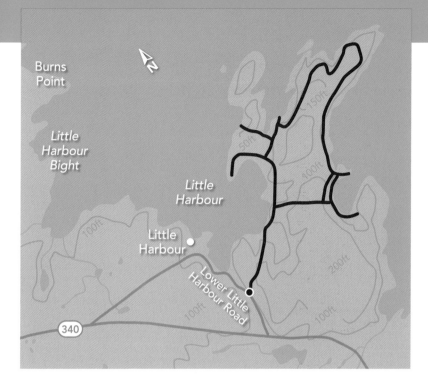

Distance:
5.5-kilometre trail network.

Trailhead access: From Route 340, turn left at the Little Harbour exit before the town of Twillingate. Within a few hundred metres, close to Atlantic View Cabins, you'll see a small parking area and trail map on the right: 49.6270344, -54.7092342.

Do not block the dirt road when parking.

Amenities: A few benches on the trail near the arch and at Jonas Cove.

Keep in mind: The trail from the arch toward Jonas Cove forces hikers to cross a narrow, rocky beach. Beware of tides and slippery wet rocks.

Permits & fees: Donations toward trail upkeep are payable to the Town of Twillingate.

⭐ Don't miss the natural arch which has inspired many painters and photographers. Be sure to visit the Keefe's root cellar that dates to 1930 and was used to store potatoes, carrots, and other vegetables, acting as a refrigerator.

2 Gillard's Cove (South Twillingate Island)

Multiple signs and maps placed along the Top of Twillingate Trail ensure easy route finding. For a short, easy stroll without any elevation gain, turn left at the first opportunity past the trailhead. This trail leads onto a boardwalk around Low Mist Pond and offers opportunities to see some of Newfoundland's flora, such as the pitcher plant. This loop returns to the main trail. You may turn right and hike back to the parking lot.

If you are seeking more breathtaking views, turn left after completing the loop and head to the summit of Twillingate and an observation tower at an elevation of 100 metres. You will encounter four lookout platforms on the way to the tower, each with a view of Twillingate Island from a different angle.

Distance:
5-kilometre trail network.

Trailhead access: Take Route 340 to Twillingate Island. Turn right onto Bayview Street (1 kilometre past the bridge for Twillingate Island), and drive about 4 kilometres to Gillard's Cove. A brown garden arch and a sign mark the trailhead and small parking area: 49.6186118, -54.7529859.

Amenities: Picnic tables, benches, lookout platforms, and an observation tower along the trail.

Keep in mind: Be careful: some of the stairs may be unstable or broken.

Permits & fees: Donations toward trail upkeep are payable to the Town of Twillingate.

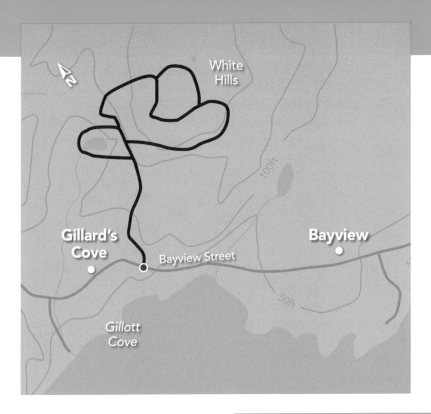

White Hills

100ft

Bayview

Gillard's Cove

Bayview Street

50ft

Gillott Cove

⭐ This trail brings you to the highest point on Twillingate Island. At an elevation of 100 metres, it offers a 360-degree panorama of Twillingate Island and Notre Dame Bay. Icebergs are sometimes seen in the distance.

2 Crow Head (North Twillingate Island)

The Long Point Lighthouse Trail starts directly behind the lighthouse; a map marks the trailhead. It meanders along the rugged coastline and sharp 300-metre-high cliffs, losing and gaining elevation at various points and, if you're lucky, offering opportunities to see whales, seabirds, and bald eagles. Devils Cove provides hikers with panoramic views of nearby islands and Notre Dame Bay.

At Horney Head Cove, head down to the beach. On the right side is a sea cave to be explored. Keep hiking toward the lookout at Cuckhold Point for a view of Twillingate Harbour. The Long Point Lighthouse will be in view during most of the hike.

From Cuckhold Point, the trail leaves the shore and leads into the forest. Hikers may return the way they came, or head toward the Wild Cove / Drong Hill trailhead or the Crow Head trailhead. If you choose Crow Head, you'll reach a high point (elevation, 76 metres) with a view of the community. Stop at the Crow's Nest Café for a smoothie or coffee. The Wild Cove trail will lead you to Drong Road.

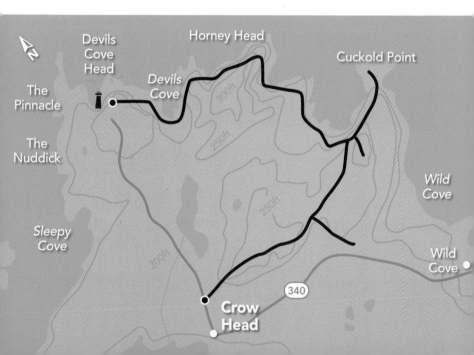

Long Point Lighthouse, built in 1876, is 100 metres above sea level. It is located on top of a cliff named Devil's Cove Head and overlooks Iceberg Alley. Visit the *Titanic* exhibit inside the lighthouse.

Distance: 5-kilometre linear trail (10-kilometre return).

Note: Combine this trail with the Long Point Lighthouse to Lower Head Trail (hike #60) to complete the loop.

Trailhead access: This trail has two trailheads:

■ Behind Long Point Lighthouse, follow Route 340 through Crow Head to Long Point Lighthouse and park: 49.6876189, -54.8009675.

■ On Main Street in Crow Head, pass Crow's Nest Café and take the first road on your right (not the one right across from the café). It is a dirt road. Park on the side of the road before you get to the first house: 49.6767782,

-54.8032394. Walk about 20 metres down a quad trail—there are no signs and the trail is a little overgrown—then turn left onto a smaller path.

Amenities: Washrooms and a gift shop which sells ice cream, drinks, and fudge at Long Point Lighthouse.

Keep in mind: If exploring the sea cave at Horney Head Cove, beware of changing tides. Stay away from cliffs, as they drop abruptly into the ocean, and gusts of wind are common. Steeper sections of the trail have loose rocks and should be hiked carefully.

Permits & fees: Donations toward trail upkeep are payable to the Town of Twillingate.

Crow Head (North Twillingate Island)

Long Point Lighthouse to Lower Head Trail is a coastal trail with short offshoot trails inland. Hikers may hike only the Lower Head loop, which offers views of Crow Head and Sleepy Cove and brings you back to your vehicle. This loop can be accessed from either Crow Head or Sleepy Cove.

Alternatively, hikers may walk all the way to the lighthouse. Sleepy Cove to Nanny's Hole has no elevation gain. Nanny's Hole lies directly underneath the impressive cliff on which Long Point Lighthouse is located, less than 1 kilometre away. The trail to Long Point Lighthouse is the only section requiring a short but steep climb. The trail is well-marked from Sleepy Cove to the lighthouse with maps and signs indicating distances.

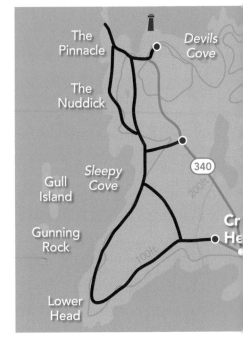

All these trails offer panoramic views of Twillingate and other islands. From the sheer cliffs along the coastline, take in the view of the ocean, and perhaps icebergs, whales, and seabirds.

Distance:
6.4-kilometre trail network.

Note: Combine this trail with the Long Point Lighthouse to Cuckhold Point Trail (hike #59) to complete the loop. This will prevent having to arrange a shuttle.

Trailhead access: Three trail access points:

■ Closest to Lower Head: In Crow Head, turn left on Broadview Street and follow it to the end (it eventually turns into a dirt road). Park by the map or cabins: 49.6767205, -54.8058554. The trail goes by cabins and then turns in to a quad trail.

■ Closest to Sleepy Cove: Before you reach Long Point Lighthouse, turn left at the hiking sign and park: 49.6831844, -54.8026623.

■ Take Route 340 to Long Point Lighthouse. Park at the lighthouse: 49.6876189, -54.8009675. The trailhead is just behind it.

Amenities: Picnic tables, and a shelter at Sleepy Cove; Long Point Lighthouse has washrooms and a gift shop.

Keep in mind: Watch out for stinging nettles—they burn the skin for a few minutes, but the sting usually diminishes quickly. Long pants are advised. Be careful when approaching cliffs, especially during high winds. If you go down to the beach at Nanny's Hole, watch for loose rocks.

Permits & fees: Donations toward trail upkeep are payable to the Town of Twillingate.

At Sleepy Cove look for an old root cellar and remnants of the copper mine that closed in 1917. Thousands of birds such as seagulls, black guillemots, terns, and puffins live on Sleepy Cove Gull Island.

Back Harbour (North Twillingate Island)

Three relatively gentle trails start in Back Harbour. Pick one for a relaxing evening stroll, or follow all three and spend a few hours exploring North Twillingate Island.

> ★ Visit Twillingate Museum for more about the history and traditions of Twillingate Island. Just beside Twillingate museum is St. Peter's Anglican Church, one of Newfoundland's oldest wooden churches.

■ Spencer's Park Trails (3.4-kilometre trail network): From Dock Road, follow the left quad trail; it will open up onto a gravel road. The trail does not involve much elevation change. You'll reach a little cove with a rocky beach—stay and watch the sunset, if the timing is right! As you head toward Spencer's Park, you'll also have views of Batrix/Barrick's Island, Back Harbour, and Notre Dame Bay.

■ Batrix/Barrick's Island Trail (1.3-kilometre linear trail): From Back Harbour wharf, head straight toward the narrow sand beach connecting Batrix/Barrick's Island to the main island. After a short climb to the summit of Batrix/Barrick's Head, you'll have views of Back Harbour, Back Harbour Bay, Dumpling Cove, and Twillingate.

■ Back Harbour to Twillingate Museum Trail (1.3-kilometre linear trail): As you leave from Twillingate Museum, you'll see Twillingate, Back Harbour, and the shoreline. You'll also encounter St. Peter's Church cemetery along the way.

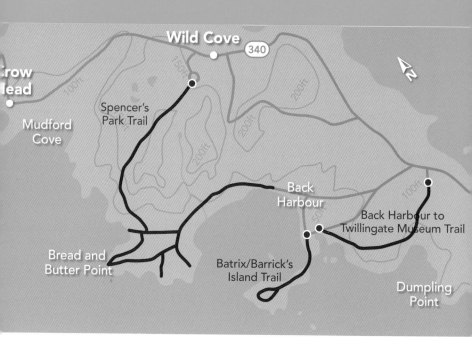

Wild Cove (340)

row
lead

Mudford
Cove

Spencer's
Park Trail

Back
Harbour

Back Harbour to
Twillingate Museum Trail

Bread and
Butter Point

Batrix/Barrick's
Island Trail

Dumpling
Point

Distance:
See hike descriptions above.

Trailhead access:

■ Spencer's Park Trails: From Route 340 (Main Street) in Wild Cove turn onto Park Street and park by the "ATVs only" sign: 49.6696438, -54.7888492.

■ Batrix/Barrick's Island Trail: From Route 340 (Main Street) in Back Harbour, take Back Harbour Road, turn left on Dock Road, and drive to the wharf: 49.6576352, -54.7891308. Park out of the way of fishing operations.

■ Back Harbour to Twillingate Museum Trail: Park in the same place as you would for Batrix/ Barrick's Island Trail or park at the Twillingate Museum and St.

Peter's Church. Hike up the dirt road and turn right before the cemetery.

Amenities: None.

Keep in mind: None of these trails have signs; if you have trouble finding the trailheads, ask local residents for assistance.

Permits & fees: Donations toward trail upkeep are payable to the Town of Twillingate.

Equipment checklist for day hikes

- [ ] Small backpack/daypack
- [ ] Water (2 to 4 litres per person per day, more in hot weather)
- [ ] Sturdy shoes or hiking boots
- [ ] Appropriate clothing (warm clothes in layers and waterproof outer layers)
- [ ] Flashlight and extra batteries
- [ ] Lighter or waterproof matches
- [ ] Fire starter
- [ ] Pocket knife
- [ ] Whistle
- [ ] Cell phone
- [ ] Snacks and lunch
- [ ] Small first-aid kit
- [ ] Sunscreen and bug repellent
- [ ] Map, GPS, and compass
- [ ] Binoculars and camera

Equipment checklist for multi-day hikes

- ❑ Large backpack
- ❑ Water (2 to 4 litres per person per day, more in hot weather) and water purification system
- ❑ Waterproof hiking boots
- ❑ Appropriate clothing (warm clothes in layers and waterproof jacket and pants)
- ❑ Flashlight and extra batteries
- ❑ Lighter or waterproof matches
- ❑ Fire starter
- ❑ Pocket knife
- ❑ Whistle
- ❑ Cell phone and/or other communication device
- ❑ Food for number of days plus 1–2 days extra
- ❑ First-aid kit
- ❑ Sunscreen and bug repellent
- ❑ Map, GPS, and compass
- ❑ Binoculars and camera
- ❑ Tent, sleeping bag, sleeping pad
- ❑ Repair kit
- ❑ Stove, fuel, pots, plates, utensils, cup, etc.
- ❑ Dry bag
- ❑ Rope and carabiners
- ❑ Hiking poles
- ❑ Toilet paper
- ❑ Toiletries
- ❑ Sandals (that can go in the water; extremely useful for around camp and for crossing rivers and streams)

Trail Completion Checklist

▨ Southwest Coast

- ❏ Harvey Trail
- ❏ Grand Bay West Trailway
- ❏ Table Mountain Trail
- ❏ Grand Codroy Way
- ❏ Starlight Trail
- ❏ Cow Hill & Beach Trail
- ❏ Boutte du Cap & Bread Crumb Trails
- ❏ Gravels Walking Trails
- ❏ Indian Head Range Trail
- ❏ Lewis Hills Trail
- ❏ Erin Mountain Trail

▨ Bay of Islands & Humber Valley

- ❏ Cedar Cove & Little Port Head Lighthouse Trails
- ❏ Bottle Cove & South Head Lighthouse Trails
- ❏ Tortoise Mountain Trail
- ❏ Copper Mine to Cape Trail
- ❏ Blow Me Down Mountain Trail
- ❏ Corner Brook Stream Walking Trails
- ❏ Humber Valley Trail
- ❏ Marble Mountain & Steady Brook Falls Trails

▨ Gros Morne National Park

- ❏ Overfalls Trail
- ❏ Trout River Pond Trail
- ❏ Green Gardens Trails
- ❏ Tablelands Trail
- ❏ Lookout Trail
- ❏ Stanleyville Trail
- ❏ Lomond River Trail
- ❏ Stuckless Pond Trail
- ❏ James Callaghan Trail (Gros Morne Mountain)
- ❏ Baker's Brook Falls Trail
- ❏ Green Point Coastal Trail
- ❏ Western Brook Pond & Snug Harbour Trails

- ❏ Long Range Traverse
- ❏ North Rim Traverse
- ❏ Cow Head Lighthouse Trail

▬ Northern Peninsula
- ❏ Devil's Bite Trail
- ❏ Indian Lookout Trail
- ❏ Point Riche Lighthouse Trail
- ❏ Englee Trail Network
- ❏ French Shore Trail
- ❏ Conche Trail Network
- ❏ Treena's Trail
- ❏ Whale Point Trail

▬ Central Newfoundland: Baie Verte & Twillingate
- ❏ Hummock Trail
- ❏ Ocean View Trail (Pacquet)
- ❏ Alexander Murray Trail
- ❏ Ocean View Trail (Jackson's Cove)
- ❏ Trail with a View
- ❏ Indian River Walking Trail
- ❏ Hazelnut Hiking & Adventure Trail
- ❏ Beothuk Hiking Trail
- ❏ Maple Ridge Hiking Trail
- ❏ Corduroy Brook Nature Trail &
  Grand Falls-Windsor Hiking Trails
- ❏ Walking Trails of Botwood
- ❏ Oceanside Nature Trail
- ❏ French Beach to Spiller's Cove Trail
- ❏ Spiller's Cove to Cod Jack's Cove Trail
- ❏ Lower Little Harbour Trail
- ❏ Top of Twillingate Trail
- ❏ Long Point Lighthouse to Cuckhold Point Trail
- ❏ Long Point Lighthouse to Lower Head Trail
- ❏ Back Harbour Trails

Further information and resources

Information is current as of publication and is subject to change.

Websites and contact information

Newfoundland Labrador Tourism
- www.newfoundlandlabrador.com/
- For short descriptions of more than 100 hikes and walks all around Newfoundland & Labrador: www.newfoundlandlabrador.com/thingstodo/hikingwalking
- contactus@newfoundlandlabrador.com
- (800) 563-6353

International Appalachian Trail of Newfoundland and Labrador (IATNL) IATNL is responsible for most of western Newfoundland's multi-day trails (including hikes 3, 4, 5, 9, 10, 14, 15, 16, 18, 20, 35, 36, and 39). Their website has full descriptions of trails; contact them for maps, GPS tracks, and boat shuttles to trailheads.
- www.iatnl.com
- info@iatnl.ca
- (709) 639-3113

Provincial Parks of Newfoundland and Labrador for information about locations, fees, and facilities at all provincial parks
- www.env.gov.nl.ca/env/parks/parks/find.html
- parksinfo@gov.nl.ca
- (709) 886-2331 (summer) or (709) 637-2040 (winter)

Provincial ferry routes, fares, and schedules (Marine Services Division, Department of Transportation and Works)
- www.tw.gov.nl.ca/ferryservices/
- (888) 638-5454

BonTours (providers of Western Brook Pond boat tour); reservations needed
- www.bontours.ca
- (888) 458-2016 or (709) 458-2016

- Visit their office at the Ocean View Motel in Rocky Harbour or dockside at Western Brook Pond

Go Western Newfoundland
- www.gowesternnewfoundland.com
- info@gowesternnewfoundland.com
- (709) 639-4787

Gros Morne National Park of Canada
- www.pc.gc.ca/eng/pn-np/nl/grosmorne
- grosmorne.info@pc.gc.ca
- (709) 458-2417

Outer Bay of Islands Enhancement Committee (OBIEC) has developed many trails in that area
- yorkharbourlarkharbour.com/Trails.htm (gives details and short videos of each trail)

Corner Brook Stream Development Corporation
- www.cbstream.com
- info@cbstream.com
- (709) 639-9266

Marble Mountain
- www.skimarble.com/page/summer-fun
- (888) 462-7253

French Shore Historical Society
- www.frenchshore.com
- frenchshorehs@nf.aibn.com
- (709) 622-3500

Port au Choix National Historic Site of Canada
- www.pc.gc.ca/eng/lhn-nhs/nl/portauchoix/index.aspx
- (709) 861-3522 (summer) or (709) 458-2417 (off-season)

Lighthouse Friends for information about lighthouses in Newfoundland and across Canada

- www.lighthousefriends.com

Corduroy Brook Enhancement Association

- www.corduroybrook.org
- corduroybrook@nf.sympatico.ca
- (709) 489-3900

Town of Triton

- www.townoftriton.ca/explore-triton/maple-ridge-hiking-trail/
- townoftriton@eastlink.ca
- (709) 263-2264

Town of Botwood

- town.botwood.nl.ca
- botwoodtowncouncil@nf.aibn.com
- (709) 257-2839

Town of Twillingate

- www.twillingate.com/toseedo/hikingwalking/
- townoftwillingate@bellaliant.com
- (709) 884-2438

Town of Springdale

- www.townofspringdale.ca/hikingTrails.html

Town of Isle aux Morts

- www.isleauxmorts.ca/hiking_trails.php
- info@isleauxmorts.ca
- (709) 698-3441

Town of Channel-Port aux Basques

- www.portauxbasques.ca/recreation/trailway
- sstrickland@portauxbasques.ca
- (709) 695-2214

Town of Springdale
- www.townofspringdale.ca/hikingTrails.html
- recreation@townofspringdale.ca or info@townofspringdale.ca
- (709) 673-3439

Town of Roberts Arm
- townofrobertsarm@eastlink.ca
- (709) 652-3331

Town of Englee
- www.engleenl.ca/attractions.html
- dorisenglee@nf.aibn.com
- (709) 866-2711

Videos (available on YouTube)

- "International Appalachian Trail Newfoundland & Labrador Movie" by Flagler Films
- "Overfalls Trail in Gros Morne National Park, Newfoundland, Canada" by Flagler Films
- "Blog: Steady Brook Falls, Newfoundland and Labrador" by Newfoundland Labrador Tourism
- "A Hike up Marble Mountain, Newfoundland and Labrador" by Peter Bull
- "Recommended Hiking Trails in Newfoundland," a blog by Keith Nicol, has descriptions and links to dozens of YouTube videos that Nicol created of the trails of western Newfoundland: www2.swgc.mun.ca/~knicol/NLhiking.htm

Recommended booklets and maps

Come Explore the Exploits Valley (2013–2014), Phoenix Publishing

Conche Trail Map, French Shore Historical Society, Quebec-Labrador Foundation

Corduroy Brook Nature Trail, Corduroy Brook Enhancement Association, Grand Falls-Windsor

The Great Northern Peninsula Trail Guide (includes many shorter trails located in the St. Anthony region and available in print at local visitor information centres)

Trails and Whales of the Great Whale Coast. (2010) Emerald Zone Corporation. Available online at www.ezc.ca/images/gallery/0000/0111/Whale_and_Trails_Web.pdf

Twillingate Map, Town of Twillingate

Welcome to Grand Falls-Windsor, Town Map

Maps used in the creation of this guide

Natural Resources Canada Toporama, retrieved May 2013 through January 2014

Photo credits

Unless otherwise indicated, numbers refer to hike numbers, not page numbers.

Katie Broadhurst: Lower front cover photos (photos 2, 3, 4), 29, 33, 37, 38, 39, 40, 41, 42

Anne Alexandra Fortin: Top front cover photo, lower front cover photo (1), back cover photos, Introduction photos, 5, 6, 7, 8, 10, 11, 12, 13, 14, 15, 16, 18 (photos 2, 3, and 4), 19, 20, 21, 22, 23, 24, 25, 26, 27, 28, 30, 31, 32, 34, 43, 44, 45, 46, 47, 48, 49, 50, 51, 52, 53, 54, 55, 56, 57, 58, 59, 60, 61

Dave Jerome: 33

Jamie Harnum and Caroline Swan: 29

Paul Wylezol: 3, 4, 35, 36, 39

Index by trail rating

The numbers that appear by hike names refer to hike numbers, not page numbers. Italics indicate the rating of a more difficult optional trail section or add-on.

Easy

Moderate trails

Baker's Brook Falls Trail 29

Boutte du Cap Trail 7

Conche Trail Network 40

Corner Brook Stream Walking Trails 17

Englee Trail Network 38

French Beach to Spiller's Cove Trail 55

Hazelnut Hiking & Adventure Trail 49

Hummock Trail 43

Indian River Walking Trail 48

Lomond River Trail 26

Long Point Lighthouse to Cuckhold Point Trail 59

Lower Little Harbour Trail 57

Maple Ridge Hiking Trail 51

Spiller's Cove to Cod Jack's Cove Trail 56

Stanleyville Trail 25

Starlight Trail 5

Stuckless Pond Trail 27

Top of Twillingate Trail 58

Treena's Trail 41

Difficult trails

Alexander Murray Trail 45

Erin Mountain Trail 11

Grand Codroy Way 4

Green Gardens Trails 22

Humber Valley Trail 18

Indian Head Range Trail 9

Little Port Head Lighthouse Trail 12

Lookout Trail 24

Marble Mountain Trail 19

Overfalls Trail 20

Snug Harbour Trail 31

South Head Lighthouse Trail 13

Starlight Trail 5

Table Mountain Trail 3

Tortoise Mountain Trail 14

Trout River Pond Trail 21

Strenuous trails
Copper Mine to Cape Trail 15
James Callaghan Trail (Gros Morne Mountain) 28

Wilderness trails
Blow Me Down Mountain Trail 16
Devil's Bite Trail 35
French Shore Trail 39
Grand Codroy Way 4
Humber Valley Trail 18
Indian Lookout Trail 36
Lewis Hills Trail 10
Long Range Traverse 32
North Rim Traverse 33
Starlight Trail 5

Index by place name

The numbers that appear by hike names refer to hike numbers, not page numbers.

About the Authors

Katie Broadhurst

Originally from Forester's Falls, Ontario, Katie began her outdoor adventure career working at Wilderness Tours on the Ottawa River. She pursued a business diploma in Outdoor Adventure Tourism at Algonquin College, which has allowed her to work and explore across Canada. Katie has been a resident of and tour guide in Newfoundland since 2009. She has worked as trail crew with IATNL, guided tours in Gros Morne National Park and up the Northern Peninsula, and explored western Newfoundland's trails year-round. She is passionate about the outdoors and thrilled to share this passion with a wider audience.

Anne Alexandra Fortin

Anne Alexandra was born and raised in the beautiful province of Quebec, where she nourished a passion for hiking and travelling. She travelled through Canada, the United States, Central America, southeast Asia, and the Chilean and Argentinean Patagonia, exploring mountains, jungles, pampas, glaciers, volcanoes, tundra, and more. These experiences inspired her to complete an Adventure Tourism Program in Gaspé, Québec. She became a professional outdoor guide and has worked from the southernmost tip of the Americas to Canada. Since 2009, she has been hiking and discovering the hidden gems of Newfoundland and Labrador's backcountry. With this book, she hopes to share the uniqueness of western and central Newfoundland with a wide audience.